*Florentino
and The Devil*

Alberto Arvelo Torrealba

FLORENTINO AND THE DEVIL

Translated by Timothy Adès
with Gloria Carnevali

FLORENTINO Y EL DIABLO

Shearsman Books

First published in the United Kingdom in 2014 by
Shearsman Books
50 Westons Hill Drive
Emersons Green
BRISTOL
BS16 7DF

Shearsman Books Ltd Registered Office
30–31 St. James Place, Mangotsfield, Bristol BS16 9JB
(this address not for correspondence)

www.shearsman.com

ISBN 978-1-84861-348-5

Cover by Cunningham Design.

ABOUT THE TEXTS

The poetry in this book, Spanish and English on facing pages, is the work of three people. The Spanish is by Alberto Arvelo Torrealba, the English is by the translator-poet Timothy Adès, a specialist in rhyme and metre. Gloria Carnevali knows the country and customs of the great plains, the quality of the people, the splendour of the flora and fauna. Her advice, unstinting andindispensable, enabled the translator to create this English text.

THE AUTHOR

Alberto Arvelo Torrealba was a lawyer, educator and poet. Born 4 September 1905 in the city of Barinas, he was a schoolboy there and went on to the Liceo in Caracas where he took his bachelor's degree in1927. He studied law in the Central University of Venezuela, qualifying as an Advocate and, in 1935, as a Doctor of Political Science.

A poet in the tradition of the "Bards of the Plains", he published his first volume of verses, *Música del Cuatro*, in 1928. A dedicated teacher, he taught Spanish Language and Literature in various Colleges and Liceos of the Metropolitan Zone, 1935-6: Sacred Heart of Jesus College, Sucre College, Polytechnic Institute, Liceo Caracas, Andrés Bello and Fermín Toro. He became Technical Inspector of secondary education in the Federal District, and of primary education in Barinas and Apure, in 1936, and was appointed Secretary of the Government of Portuguesa State, 1937, and President of the Technical Council for Education, 1940. In the same year he published his *Glosas al Cancionero*, a model of poetry with popular roots which also contained the first version of his poem *Florentino y el Diablo*. In 1941-44 he was President of the State of Barinas. While in office, he had the riverbeds of the Pagüey and the Masparro dredged, and restored the trading routes in the Western Plains region. A member of the Court of Appeal, 1948, Ambassador of Venezuela in Bolivia, 1951-2, and in Italy, 1952, he was then Minister of Agriculture and Stockbreeding, 1952-5. Retiring from politics, he devoted himself to his profession and his literary calling. He published a study of the poet Francisco Lazo Martí (of the State of Guárico) in 1965, followed by that poet's *Collected Poetic Works* in 1967. His own translations of Giuseppe Ungaretti appeared in 1969. On 31 May 1968 he became a member of the Academia Venezolana de la Lengua. He died in Caracas on 28 March 1971.

The principal works of Arvelo Torrealba include: *Caminos que Andan; Cantas: Poemas; Florentino y el Diablo; Lazo Martí: Vigencia en Lejanía; Música de Cuatro;* and *Obra Poética.* In 1974 Orlando Araujo published a book on Arvelo Torrealba called *Contrapunto de la Vida y Muerte: ensayo sobre la poesía de Alberto Arvelo Torrealba.*

THE TRANSLATOR
Timothy Adès is a British translator-poet who works with rhyme and metre. He won the *Times Literary Supplement* Premio Valle-Inclán Prize for his version of Homero en Cuernavaca by the Mexican poet, Alfonso Reyes, and has awards for translations of the French poets Victor Hugo, Jean Cassou and Robert Desnos. Volumes of these poets are published or forthcoming. He translates from German and Greek, especially the poems of Brecht and Sikelianós. He is in demand at festivals and poetry nights, and runs a bookstall of poetry in translation.

THE VENEZUELAN CONSULTANT
Gloria Carnevali, formerly a curator at the Museo de Arte Contemporáneo in Caracas, director of the Galeria de Arte Moderno Jesús Soto at Ciudad Bolívar in Venezuela, a research fellow at Clare Hall, Cambridge and Cultural Attaché at the Venezuelan Embassy in London, has written two books on the philosophy of art, and translated for the Cambridge University Press. She has travelled throughout Venezuela studying the folklore, customs and music of the people, and coordinated programmes on the Venezuelan *llanos* for BBC radio and television. She now lives and writes in England.

Thanks are due to the Arvelo family, and to Sacven.

"...Florentino the Araucan, the great Singer of the Plain who expressed everything in verse, and whom even The Devil himself could not vanquish in the contest to see which could improvise the most, one night when he came disguised as a Christian: Florentino's voice was giving out, but his well of inspiration was still running over, and when it was almost time for the cocks to crow, mentioning the Holy Trinity in a stanza, he drove his opponent back into Hell, head over heels with his rattle and everything."

—Rómulo Gallegos, *Doña Bárbara*
(Rómulo Gallegos became President of Venezuela.)

"...I found the most beautiful lands in the world. I arrived there one day before noon, and seeing this verdure and this beauty, I decided to cast anchor and to see the inhabitants..."

—Christopher Columbus in 1499,
referring to territory now occupied by
Venezuela, which he called *Tierra de Gracia*.

Florentino y el Diablo

Florentino and The Devil

El reto

El coplero Florentino
por el ancho terraplén
caminos del Desamparo
desanda a golpe de seis.
Puntero en la soledad
que enlutan llamas de ayer,
macolla de tierra errante
le nace bajo el corcel.
Ojo ciego el lagunazo   10
sin junco, garza ni grey,
dura cuenca enterronada
donde el casco da traspié.
Los escuálidos espinos
desnudan su amarillez,
las chicharras atolondran
el cenizo anochecer.
Parece que para el mundo
la palma sin un vaivén.
El coplero solitario   20
vive su grave altivez
de ir caminando el erial
como quien pisa vergel.
En el caño de Las Ánimas
se para muerto de sed
y en las patas del castaño
ve lo claro del jagüey.
El cacho de beber tira,
en agua lo oye caer;
cuando lo va levantando   30
se le salpican los pies,
pero del cuerno vacío
ni gota pudo beber.
Vuelve a tirarlo y salpica

The Challenge

Florentino, poet and singer,
at the sixth peal rides again
down the trails of Misadventure
on the broad unflooded plain.
Cattle-herd of the lonesome vastness,
clad in black by the flames that charred,
loose earth at his horse's footfall
rises up in a dusty cloud.
A sightless eye is the lochan,
no heron nor herd nor reed:
with clods the ground is littered
to trip the stumbling steed.
The sorry buckthorn bushes
are faded and bare and stark,
the drone of crickets weighs heavy
on the gathering ashen dark.
It seems that the world has halted,
no breeze in the palm is seen:
all alone is the craftsman of verses,
in his lofty pride serene,
travelling over the wild lands
as if in a garden green.
At the runnel of Las Ánimas
he has halted, dying of thirst:
he sees the foot of his chestnut horse
in the shining pool immersed.
His drinking-horn he has lowered,
in the water he hears it fall;
he draws it up, and it spatters
his feet, dripping sweet and small:
yet from the empty vessel
he can drink no drop at all.
Again he throws, and clear water

el agua clara otra vez:
ávido sorbo susurran
los belfos del palafrén;
dulce rosario destila
del empapado cordel;
mas sólo arena los ojos   40
en el turbio fondo ven.
Soplo de quema el suspiro,
dobladas espigas sin mies,
la sabia ardiendo en la imagen
de nunca reverdecer,
mirada y rumbo el coplero
pone para su caney
cuando con trote sombrío
oye un jinete tras él.
Negra se le ve la manta,   50
negro el caballo también;
bajo el negro pelo'e guama
la cara no se le ve.
Pasa cantando en romance
sin la mirada volver:
"En negra orilla del mundo
se han de hallar de quien a quien
aquél que ve sin mirar
y aquél que mira sin ver.
Cuando esté más hondo el río   60
aguárdeme en Santa Inés,
que yo lo voy a buscar
para cantar con usté.
Soy retador de juglares
desde los siglos del rey.
Le sobra con esperarme
si me quiere conocer."

Mala sombra del espanto
cruza por el terraplén:
hacia mármoles de ocaso   70

spatters him once again:
the dry lips of the palfrey
hum with a thirsty refrain.
Sweet rosaries of droplets
drip from the well-drenched string;
when he gazes deep in the vessel,
sand, sand is the only thing.
His brow and his breath are burning
like wilted stalks with no grain,
the very sap boils, you imagine
it will never grow green again.
To his home and cabin the Rhymer
has turned his course and his mind,
when he hears the sinister hoofbeat
of a horseman trotting behind.
Black to behold is the poncho,
black is the horse withal;
under the black sombrero
the face was not seen at all
The horseman goes singing a ballad,
he does not turn his eye:
'On the world's black edge we must measure
man against man, you and I.
One of us sees without looking,
one looks but he does not see:
At Santa Inés, when the river
is deep, pray wait for me.
I would seek you out to try you,
and with you I would sing.
I have contended with jesters
from the centuries of the king.
Attend me there, you shall know me,
you shall have your reckoning.'

The spectre's evil shadow
sweeps over the mighty plain:
long as a cypress it stretches

se alarga como un ciprés.
Jinetes de lejanía
la acompañan en tropel;
la encobijan y la borran
pajas del anochecer.
Florentino taciturno
coge el banco de través.
Puntero en la soledad
que enlutan llamas de ayer
caminante sin camino,   80
resero sin una res,
parece que va soñando
con la sabana en la sien.
En un verso largo y hondo
se le estira el tono fiel,
con su América andaluza
en lo español barinés:
"Sabana, sabana, tierra
que hace sudar y querer,
parada con tanto rumbo,   90
con agua y muerta de sed.
Una con mi alma en lo sola,
una con Dios en la fe;
sobre tu pecho desnudo
yo me paro a responder.
Sepa el cantador sombrío
que yo cumplo con mi ley
y como canté con todos
tengo que cantar con él".

to the bloodshot dying sun.
Riding abroad with the spectre
goes a troop of horsemen afar:
by slivers of night they are hidden,
in the dusk they disappear.
Florentino silent and brooding
turns his course away to the side.
Cattle-herd of the lonesome vastness,
clad in black by the flames that charred,
a man of the road, but of no road,
a herdsman without a herd,
it seems that he goes dreaming,
the savannah is in his brain:
he sings a song, tuned truly,
a long and a deep refrain
of his Andaluz America,
of Barinas, language of Spain:
'Savannah, my savannah,
land sweated for and loved,
unmoving in all directions,
watered and water-starved:
one with my soul in aloneness,
one in the faith with the Lord:
on your naked breast I have halted,
this answer I record.
Let him know, the shadowy singer,
I am a man of my word:
I who have sung with all men,
with him shall my voice be heard.'

Santa Inés

Noche de fiero chubasco
por la enlutada llanura,
y de encendidas chipolas
que el rancho del peón alumbran.
Adentro suena el capacho,
afuera bate la lluvia.
Vena en corazón de cedro
el bordón mana ternura.
No lejos asoma el río
pecho de sabana sucia.   110
Inmóviles carameras
pávidos brazos desnudan.
Escombro de minas lóbregas
el trueno arrastra y derrumba.
Más allá coros errantes,
ventarrón de negra furia.
Y mientras se duerme el son
en las cuerdas vagabundas
el rayo a la palma sola
le tira señeras puntas.   120
Canta una voz sabanera
por el pensamiento pura,
por la ilusión cristalina,
por el aguardiente turbia:
"Piqué con la medianoche
cimarroneras en fuga:
le eché soga a un orejano
y enlacé la media luna.
"Después cruzando sediento
sobre la arena desnuda   130
vide la tierra estrellada
con lirios de primer lluvia.
"Y como si todo fuera
por caprichos de fortuna,
le abrí mi lazo al amor:

Santa Inés

Night of a fearsome cloudburst
over the black-garbed plain:
candles burn in rough holders,
lighting a humble domain:
indoors, the sounding maracas,
outdoors, the pounding rain.
The harp is heart-vein of cedar,
its burden is low and sweet.
The river bathes the savannah,
cleansing its breast of the dirt.
The rooted trees have antlers
that are terrified arms, stripped bare;
the thunder disturbs dark tailings,
hurling them everywhere.
There's many a moaning chorus,
black fury of storms that stray;
The wandering harpstrings slacken,
the music has died away,
and the lonely palm is stricken
with bolts of the lightning-ray.
A voice of the savannah
sings, pure in thought, transparent,
crystal-clear in suggestion,
rough and raw with liquid spirit.
"At midnight I have herded
the runaway cimarrón:
aimed my rope at a beast unbranded
and captured the bright half-moon.
"I journeyed then dry-throated
on the bare sandy plain:
I saw the land star-studded
with lilies of fresh first rain.
"It may be our fortunes are settled
by a fate that's whimsical:
I cast my lasso for loving,

sólo enlacé la amargura.
"Desde entonces en mi libro
hay no más que dos pinturas:
el chaparro en la candela
y el pimpollo en la garúa.   140
"Por eso sé distinguir
en los ayes que te cruzan,
montaña de Santa Inés,
clamor de la gente tuya:
Fusileros federales
en godas cabalgaduras
anunciando la pelea:
la del siempre con el nunca."
Súbito un hombre en la puerta:
indio de grave postura,   150
ojos negros, pelo negro,
frente de cálida arruga,
pelo de guama luciente
que con el candil relumbra,
faja de hebilla lustrosa
con letras que se entrecruzan,
mano de sobrio tatuaje,
lunar de sangre en la nuca.
Un golpe de viento guapo
le pone a volar la blusa,   160
y se le ve jeme y medio
de puñal en la cintura.
Entra callado y se apuesta
para el lado de la música.
Dos dientes de oro le aclaran
la sonrisa taciturna.
"Oiga, vale, ése es el Diablo"
la voz por la sala cruza.
Fíjese cómo llegó,
sin cobija ni montura,   170
planchada y seca la ropa,
con tanto barrial y lluvia

caught bitterness, that was all.
"From that day on, two pictures
are all that my book displays:
the bud of a flower in the drizzle,
the evergreen oak ablaze.
"That is how I distinguish,
when I hear the clamours warring
on your high ground, Santa Inés,
your own true people's cheering:
The Federals firing volleys
as the Gothic cavalry charges,
proclaiming the struggle's fury:
Forever against Nevermore!"
See now, a man at the door!
An Indian, grave his bearing,
swarthy his eyes and skin,
his brow furrowed with cunning.
In the light of the candles
the man's sombrero glitters:
on his waist-sash, shiny buckle
and interlacing letters.
On his neck a mole of blood,
sober tattoo on his hand:
then up flies his blouse
with a strong gust of wind,
revealing at his belt
a dagger, nine inches long.
Silent he enters, and stands
where the music beckons to song.
A couple of golden teeth
lighten his taciturn smile.
"Look, man, it's the Devil"
the word goes round the hall.
"Think of how he arrived,
no poncho and no steed:
his clothes are pressed and dry,
for all the rain and the mud:

alpargatas nuevecitas,
relucientes de negrura.
Dicen que pasó temprano,
como quien viene de Nutrias,
con un oscuro bonguero
por el paso de Las Brujas".
Florentino está silbando
sones de añeja bravura   180
y su diestra echa a volar
ansias que pisa la zurda,
sol menor de soledades
que los dedos desmenuzan
cuando el indio pico de oro
con su canto lo saluda:

EL DIABLO
Catire quita pesares,
contésteme esta pregunta:
¿Cuál es el gallo   190
que siempre lleva
ventaja en la lucha
y aunque le den en el pico
tiene picada segura?

FLORENTINO
Tiene picada segura
el gallo que se rebate
y no se atraviesa nunca,
bueno si tira de pie,
mejor si pica en la pluma.   200

EL DIABLO
Mejor si pica en la pluma.
Si sabe tanto de todo diga
¿cuál es la república
donde el tesoro es botín
sin dificultá ninguna?

with new little espadrilles
polished black, he's neatly shod.
They say he came here before,
as if from Waterdog City,
with a shadowy boatman
by way of the Pass of Witches."
Florentino is whistling
songs of old bravery:
his right hand soars with yearning,
his left plucks pensively:
his fingers shred his longing
in the mournful minor key,
when the Indian accosts him,
golden-tongued, with melody:

THE DEVIL
Lily-face, Jovial Jack!
Now, answer me back:
What fighting-cock
takes a trick in the ruck,
the cock of the walk:
though struck in the beak,
he makes a good peck?

FLORENTINO
He makes a good peck,
the cock who tracks back
and doesn't lash back,
keeps his feet, or still better
he pecks the cock-feather.

THE DEVIL
He pecks the cock-feather.
If you're such a know-all,
say, what's the republic
whose treasure is nobbled
without any trouble?

FLORENTINO
Sin dificultá ninguna
la colmena en el papayo,
que es palo de blanda pulpa: 210
el que no carga machete
saca la miel con las uñas.

EL DIABLO
Saca la miel con las uñas.
Respóndame la tercera
si contestó la segunda:
¿Cuáles son los cuatro ríos
que llevan la misma ruta,
silentes si no los pasan,
sonoros cuando los cruzan?   220

FLORENTINO
Sonoros cuando los cruzan.
Las cuatro cuerdas del cuatro
en pecho de quien las pulsa;
salpica el tono en el traste
como en la piedra la espuma.
El que interroga se enreda
en sus propias conjeturas
si el que aprendió a responder
juega con la repregunta.   230

EL DIABLO
Juega con la repregunta.
Defiéndase de la cuarta
si tiene tanta facundia:
¿Quién sin látigo ni espuela,
jinete, la marcha apura
sobre el que no da caballo
pero sí puede dar mula?

FLORENTINO
Without any trouble,
a hive, up a pawpaw's
trim trunk of weak timber:
without a machete
bare hands claw the honey.

THE DEVIL
Bare hands claw the honey.
You answered that query:
for this one, be canny.
What quartet of waters
all follow one route,
are mute if unmet,
yet loud in the moot?

FLORENTINO
Yet loud in the moot,
cuatrista's quartet,
four strings, on his heart:
as spindrift a stone,
tone spatters the fret.
The asker is snared,
caught out in his guessing,
by one who's prepared
to play counter-question.

THE DEVIL
To play counter-question.
So skilful of speech!
Watch out for the fourth:
Who quickens his course,
without whip or spur,
on what sires no horse
but a mule it may sire?

FLORENTINO
Pero sí puede dar mula.   240
Esa pregunta retrata
en pelo como en jamugas
al muchacho que va al trote
y acelera por la grupa
si le hace al burro cosquillas
donde fue la matadura.

EL DIABLO
Donde fue la matadura.
 Le prevengo que la quinta
lleva veneno en la punta: 250
dígame si anduvo tanta
sabana sin sol ni luna:
¿quién es el que bebe arena
en la noche más oscura?

FLORENTINO
En la noche más oscura
no ando escondiendo mi sombra
ni me espanto de la suya.
Lo malo no es el lanzazo
sino quien no lo retruca.   260
Sobre los suelos errantes,
bajo la sed de las dunas,
por la ribera del mar
y en la mar de estas llanuras
cuando se quema hasta el aire
y se tuesta la laguna
tiene que beber arena
el que no bebe agua nunca.

EL DIABLO
El que no bebe agua nunca.   270
No me termine el velorio,

FLORENTINO
But a mule it may sire.
This query's depicting
some lad who's trit-trotting,
bareback or on sacking,
who quickens his jackass
by tickling its carcase
on the bite or the sore.

THE DEVIL
On the bite or the sore.
The fifth now: be warned
of poison-tipped pain.
You roamed on the plain
with no sun nor moon:
who drinks down the sand
in the night's darkest hour?

FLORENTINO
In the night's darkest hour
I don't hide my shadow
nor shudder at yours:
unhurt by your spear
I fling it back at you.
On wandering sands,
down waterless dunes,
along the sea-strands,
in seas of the plains,
when the very air burns
and the waterhole's seared:
there's one must drink sand,
who never drinks water.

THE DEVIL
Who never drinks water.
Don't scupper my send-off

ligando el café con brusca,
que murciélago no es pájaro
ni papelón es azúcar.
Si sabe, dé su razón;
y si no, no dé ninguna:
¿Quién en el zumo salobre
de la zábila se endulza?
¿Quién mitiga el fuego amargo
en jagüey de arena pura?   280
¿Quién mata la sed sin agua
en la soledad profunda?

FLORENTINO
En la soledad profunda,
el pecho del medanal,
el romance que lo arrulla,
la tronada que lo abisma,
el ánima que lo cruza,
el humo que lo encobija,
el soplo que lo desnuda,   290
la queja que lo salmodia,
la candela que lo enluta,
la palma que lo atalaya,
el lucero que lo alumbra,
la esperanza que lo siembra,
el dolor que lo fecunda.
¿Qué culpa tengo, señores,
si me encuentra el que me busca?

El Diablo cambia la rima

EL DIABLO   300
Si me encuentra el que me busca
el susto lo descarea.
Falta un cuarto pa'la una
cuando el candil parpadea,
cuando despúes del chubasco

with chaff in the coffee.
A bat is no bird,
raw cane is no sugar.
If you know, give your answer,
if not, then give none, sir.
Whose sweet treat's the liquor
of salt aloe vera?
Who cools fire too bitter
in pools of pure sand?
Who's slaked without water
in the deep lonesome land?

FLORENTINO
In the deep lonesome land,
the breast of the dunes
is lulled by romance,
is startled by thunder,
is crossed by a soul,
is swaddled by fumes,
is stripped by the blast,
is racked by the dirge,
is charred by the flame,
is watched by the palm,
is lit by the star,
is seeded by hope,
is fertile with pain.
Sirs, shall I be blamed,
if the seeker shall find me?

The Devil changes the rhyme

THE DEVIL
If the seeker shall find me,
then fear cracks him open.
In midnight's small hours
when candle-flames gutter
and after fierce showers

la rama triste gotea,
cuando el espanto sin rumbo
pesaroso sabanea,
cuando el ñénguere da el tono
y la guacaba solfea,   310
cuando mi aliento es la mar
y mi grito es la marea,
cuando Florentino calla
porque se le va la idea,
cuando canta la pavita,
cuando el gallo menudea.

FLORENTINO
Cuando el gallo menudea
la garganta se me afina
y el juicio se me clarea   320
como el agua manadora
que alumbrando gorgorea.
Con la lección del turpial
pulo el canto en la pelea;
y con la del espinito
que en ceja 'e monte florea
le doy aroma al que pasa
y espino al que me menea.

EL DIABLO
Espino al que me menea.   330
No le envidio al espinito
las galas de que alardea:
cuando la candela pasa
la pata se le negrea;
creciente inunda su sombra,
hormiga lo amarillea,
cigarrón chupa sus flores,
bachaco anida en su brea,
verano le tumba la hoja,
huracán lo zarandea.   340

the branches drip drooping,
when woebegone spectres
stravaig the savannah,
when plover sings shrill,
guacaba sings shriller:
deep sea is my breathing,
flood-tide is my roaring:
that's when Florentino
is silenced and failing,
when gwan-bird cries ruin,
When rooster cries morning.

FLORENTINO
When rooster cries morning
my throat sings more finely,
my thoughts come out shining
as water comes finding
the light with a gurgle.
My song's honed by jousting,
that's the troupial's lesson:
I give, like the buckthorn
in bloom on the mountain,
sweet scent if you're passing,
sharp point, if I'm shaken.

THE DEVIL
Sharp point, if I'm shaken.
I don't envy the buckthorn
that flaunts its fine fashion:
at the coming of fire
its nether parts blacken;
the floods drown its shadow,
the ants turn it yellow,
its bloom suckles crickets,
its juice draws red giants,
drought rips off its leaves, and
the hurricane blasts it.

FLORENTINO
Huracán lo zarandea.
El asta siempre está firme
cuando el pabellón ondea.
Si el despecho lo atolondra
tómese esta panacea:
prefiero entenderle al mudo
y no al que tartamudea.
Loro con ala cortada
es el que más aletea.   350
¡Quién ha visto indio en Guayana
lavando oro sin batea!
¡Quién ha visto peón de llano
que ni enlaza ni colea!
Le dijo la negra Clara
a la catira Matea:
"Si no va a comprar los gofios,
¿pa' qué me los manosea?"
Yo que le atravieso el golpe
y el arpa que bordonea.   360

EL DIABLO
Y el arpa que bordonea.
Si porque tuerce clavijas
presume tanta ralea,
ya yo le voy a enseñar
cómo el traste se puntea,
haciéndole las escalas
en fusa y semircorchea.
También le araño la armónica
por muy abajo que sea,   370
como le subo quintales
sin mecate y sin polea
y le conozco el gritico
del que eriza y cacarea.
Gallero que entiende su arte
amolando se recrea:

FLORENTINO

The hurricane blasts it.
The mast will stand fast
when the standard is waving.
Do my words drive you dizzy?
try this for your saving:
I like a mute better
than a stumbler who stutters.
Clip the wings of a parrot,
he furiously flutters.
Do tribes in Guayana
wash gold with no pail?
Can't plainsmen lasso, nor
catch bulls by the tail?
Says pretty black Clara
to pretty blonde Mattie:
"If you aren't a fair payer,
don't touch my cheese flatties!"
I've shot this across you
as the harp hums and judders.

THE DEVIL

As the harp hums and judders.
You're just a peg-twister.
Presumptuous bluster!
You'll see how I finger
the fret! I build ladders
of quavers and semis,
of semis and demis;
harmoniously spider
to lowest notes ever;
lift hundredweights higher
with no rope nor pulley.
I know too the squawk
of the goose-pimpled cluck:
the proper cock-fighter
likes making spurs sharper:

31

sabe que con bulla de ala
no se cobra la pelea;
se cobra con puñalada
cuando la sangre chorrea,   380
cuando el vencedor se empina
y el vecino patalea.
Vaya poniéndose alante
pa' que en lo oscuro me vea.

FLORENTINO
Pa' que en lo oscuro me vea.
No arrime tanto el caballo,
que el toro se le chacea.
Por derecho le salí
como le toca al que arrea   390
y usté va por travesía
cuando no me culebrea.
Atrás y alante es lo mismo
pa'l que no carga manea:
el de atrás coge respiro
cuando el de alante jadea,
el que va atrás ve pá'lante
y el que va alante voltea.

EL DIABLO
El que va alante voltea   400
a gritarle que se apure
a quien nunca se aparea
y a contemplar lo que sube
borrando lo que verdea:
en invierno el aguazal,
en verano la humarea.
Me gusta cantar al raso
de noche cuando ventea
cuando presagian diluvio
los sapos en asamblea,   410
y sus sones disonantes

he knows flapping feathers
won't carry the battle:
it's done by the stabbing
that sets the blood spurting,
that sets the cock strutting,
the local bird struggling.
Come stand here before me,
in the dark you shall see me.

FLORENTINO
In the dark you shall see me.
Don't ride your horse close
to the bull's vicious veering.
I've passed it straight on,
to catch hold at high speed:
you go right across me,
I'd say you are swerving.
Front and back are all one,
if no leading-rein's on:
front man breathing hard,
back man, second wind:
back man gazing forward,
front man's on the swivel.

THE DEVIL
Front man's on the swivel
and tells him, keep moving!
He never draws level
to see things arriving:
in spring it's the greening,
in winter the flooding,
the smoke in the summer.
I sing in the open
at night when it's windy,
when floods are foreboded,
when frogs raise together
their dissonant racket

colman la oscura platea,
porque así es como se sabe
quién mejor contrapuntea.

FLORENTINO
Quien mejor contrapuntea
hace sus tratos de día
y trabaja por tarea,
sin andar averiguando
si el caballo corcovea,   420
ni si el patrón tiene hatajo
y dónde lo veranea,
ni si a la mona le gusta
el panal de matajea,
ni los ungüentos del brujo
faculto en farmacopea
con nervios de terecay
y corazón de hicotea,
ni si se roba el novillo
el que lo cachilapea,   430
ni quien desuella la vaca
ni quien pica la correa,
ni quien siembra los guayabos,
ni quien saca la jalea,
"¡Cójame ese trompo en la uña
a ver si taratatea!".
Ni que yo fuera lechuza
en campanario de aldea
para cantar en lo oscuro
con esta noche tan fea.   440

EL DIABLO
Con esta noche tan fea
el destino de mi sombra
con el suyo se carea.
La ley por la que yo cobro,
si el fallido regatea,

that fills the dark theatre:
that's how we discover
which songster is better.

FLORENTINO
Which songster is better:
the one who deals daily
to barter his labour,
not poking his nose in
if broncos are bucking,
if bosses drive droves
off somewhere for summer,
if a she-monkey fancies
the honeybee's comb, or
a medicine-man
brews potions of turtle
with terecay tendon
or hiccatee heart, or
if that man's a thief
lassoing that calf, or
who skinned the cow's collar,
cut strips off its belly,
who's sowing the guavas,
who's reaping the jelly:
"Touch my top as it spins:
is it stumbling or steady?"
Don't think I'm an owl
in some village belfry
to sing in the dark
on a night that's so filthy.

THE DEVIL
On a night that's so filthy,
the doom of my shadow
squares off with your own, sir.
By my harsh law I harry
the paltering debtor

echándosela de libre
el que nació con librea,
ni da plazo, ni da quita,
ni avala, ni prorratea.   450
No se cancela en un día
lo que por vida flaquea.
Mercaderes del milagro
contra huracán y marea
besan el escapulario
cuando el bongo se voltea.
Se acuerdan de Santa Bárbara
sólo si relampaguea.

FLORENTINO
Sólo si relampaguea.   460
Se le ve lo mal que canta
por lo bien que sermonea.
Estúdiese esta cartilla
a ver si la deletrea:
el barco en mitad del río,
el humo en la chimenea,
el pozo en el morichal
donde el suspiro sombrea.
A la luz de la razón
no hay bulto que yo no vea   470
aunque usted con su malicia
levante esa polvarea.
Siendo bien mansa la mula
no importa si lo patea.

Coplero que canta y toca

EL DIABLO
No importa si lo patea.
Una cosa piensa el burro
y otra el que no se le apea.

who's born into service
but acts like a master:
no grace, no remitting,
no loans, no pro rata.
A lifetime of slackness,
one day cannot alter.
It's miracle-mongers
in high wind and water
kiss relics, capsizing:
the saint, they forget her,
St Barbara's missing,
till the flash and the thunder.

FLORENTINO
Till the flash and the thunder.
We know the bad singer:
he's such a good preacher.
Just study this primer
and try to decipher:
the boat on swift river,
the smoke in the chimney,
the palms by the water
that shadow and whisper.
By reason's clear lantern
I see every hazard
though you with your cunning
raise dust for a cover.
Molly Mule is no mustang,
her kick doesn't matter.

A poet who sings and plays

THE DEVIL
Her kick doesn't matter.
The jackass thinks one thing,
rough-rider another.

¡Ay, catire Florentino!   480
escuche a quien lo previene:
déle tregua a la porfía
pá'que tome y se serene,
para que el ron le de alivio
y el dolor no lo envenene
cuando el lóbrego eslabón
de la sombra lo encadene.

FLORENTINO
De la sombra lo encadene.
Por mi suerte no se apure   490
ni por mis males se apene
porque yo nunca he metido
mi cuchara en sus sartenes.
Aunque de veras le guste
la caña con kerosene,
y el mato de agua lo guise
y la iguana la rellene,
no me importa lo que tome,
señor, ni con lo que cene.
Me es igual si me calla   500
o la inspiración le viene.

EL DIABLO
O la inspiración le viene.
Inspiración se marchita
en quien humor se reviene.
Discurso fino en lisonja
asegura parabienes.
Arte sin pueblo se esfuma
como el humo de los trenes:
sólo con huella en lo que arde   510
levanta polvo en las sienes,
como ala de remolino
torcida en los terraplenes.

Fair-face Florentino!
Take heed of this warning:
back down from your bile,
drink deep and be mellow:
here's rum to relieve you
from poison of sorrow,
from dolorous chains
that shackle in shadow.

FLORENTINO
That shackle in shadow.
Don't fret for my fate,
don't sigh for my sorrow,
I never have dipped
my spoon in your skillet.
You may sip kerosene
with your sugar-spirit,
may stuff the iguana
and stew the pond-lizard,
it's all one to me, sir,
what goes in your gizzard:
all one if you falter
or quip like a wizard.

THE DEVIL
Or quip like a wizard.
Word-wizardry fades
with failing of mood.
Fine flattering words
are safely approved.
Art fades without folk
like the smoke from a train:
it must tread the hot earth,
raising dust for the brain,
like the wing of a wind
as it whirls on the plain.

FLORENTINO
Torcida en los terraplenes,
orillas del verde Arauca
llamarada se detiene
y espantados de lejura
se relinchan los palafrenes.
Burro no toca la flauta   520
ni que la flauta le suene.
A mí nunca me atajaron
en resguardos ni retenes.
Mostrencos como orejanos
yo los distingo entre cienes.
El que lleva contrabando
no pisa mis almacenes.

EL DIABLO
No pisa mis almacenes.
En comercio no se sabe   530
quién les da lección a quiénes:
si el que registra escritura
 donde traspasa sus bienes,
o quien queda propietario,
amo de lo que no tiene.
Ni chanzas dicen amores,
ni seriedad son desdenes.
Veremos si no le falla
la voz cuando se condene.

FLORENTINO   540
La voz cuando se condene.
Mientras el cuatro me afine
y la maraca resuene,
no hay espuela que me apure
ni bozal que me sofrene,
ni quien me obligue a beber
en tapara que otro llene,
ni me haga arrollar las mangas

FLORENTINO
As it whirls on the plain:
at Arauca's green banks
a fire is contained,
and far-distant horses
neigh loudly, afraid.
If an ass blows a flute
does he know how it's played?
I was never controlled,
corralled or detained:
I can pick among hundreds
wild cattle from branded:
and goods contrabanded
aren't my stock-in-trade.

THE DEVIL
Aren't my stock-in-trade.
In the hard school of business
we don't know who's learning:
the one who makes over
his assets by signing,
or the one who takes over
and finds himself owning.
Light laughs are not loving,
grave glances not spurning.
We'll see if you're losing
that voice, come the damning.

FLORENTINO
That voice, come the damning.
When my cuatro's in tune
and I hear the maracas,
no hotspur can speed me,
no halter restrain,
no man make me drain
another man's liquors,
or roll back my sleeves

habiendo tantos jejenes.
Coplero que canta y toca   550
su justa ventaja retiene:
toca cuando le da gana,
canta cuando le conviene.

EL DIABLO
Canta cuando le conviene.
Si su destino es porfiar
aunque llueva y aunque truene
le voy a participar,
amigo, que en este duelo
yo no le vengo a brindar   560
miel de aricas con buñuelo;
vengo a probarle quien soy
por los bloques que cincelo
 por los filos que he mellado
por las lomas que anhelo
yo le confirmo lo fallo
y lo firme se lo apelo.
Si se pone malicioso
no me extraña su recelo,
que al que lo mordió macagua   570
bejuco le para el pelo.

FLORENTINO
Bejuco le para el pelo.
Regaños no son castigos
ni guáimaros caramelo.
Usted manda en su trapiche
yo mi caña la muelo.
Entre cantadores canto,
entre machos me rebelo,
en quien sabe me confío   580
y del que no me conduelo,
entre palos no me gusta
por lo vidrioso el ciruelo,

when the air's full of midges.
Who both sings and plays
retains the advantage,
he plays when he pleases,
he sings when he wishes.

THE DEVIL
He sings when he wishes.
If your pathway is pride
come rain and come thunder,
I tell you, my friend,
that in this encounter
I'm not here to stand you
wild honey and yucca,
but to show you my nature
by the rasps I have blunted,
the blocks I have chiselled,
the hillsides I've levelled,
confounding all firmness,
confirming all failure.
You may turn malicious,
you're frightened, no wonder:
your snake-bite was vicious,
you dread the liana.

FLORENTINO
You dread the liana.
Mere growls are not drubbings,
A toffee's no bullet.
You run your own boilings,
My sugar, I'll mill it.
I sing among singers,
fight back among bullies,
I trust one who's canny:
one who isn't, I pity.
My timber's not little
brown willow, too brittle:

entre mujeres me sobra
muselina y terciopelo,
cuando una me dice adiós
a otra le pido consuelo,
si una me niega bizcocho
otra me da bizcochuelo.
Desde cuando yo volaba   590
paraparas del rayuelo
vide con la noche oscura
la Cruz de Mayo en el cielo.

EL DIABLO
La Cruz de Mayo en el cielo.
A mí no me espantan sombras
ni con luces me desvelo.
Con el sol soy gavilán
y en la oscuridá mochuelo;
familia de alcaraván   600
canto mejor cuando vuelo;
voy como el garzón gabán
por el humo contra el suelo
si pico como el alacrán
pregona el ¡ay! lo que duelo;
también como la guabina
si me agarra me le pelo.
Le ronco de palo en palo
como el araguato en celo
también soy caimán cebao   610
que en boca'e caño lo velo.

FLORENTINO
Que en boca'e caño lo velo.
Velando al que nunca pasa
el vivo se quedó lelo.
Velando al que nunca pasa
me acordé de aquel corrío

44

for women, I've had it
with muslins and velvets:
if one says goodbyes,
another's my solace:
if one grudges pies,
another gives patties.
Ever since I rolled cobnuts,
played tiddlywink ringers,
I've seen it on dark nights,
the May Cross in heaven.

THE DEVIL
The May Cross in heaven.
No shadows can scare me,
no lights keep awake.
In the sun I'm a hawk,
fierce red owl in the dark:
I'm stone-curlew's kin,
I sing better in flight;
I go like great ibis
through smoke, my head lowered;
I sting like a scorpion,
my hurt victims holler;
like wriggly guabina
you grasp me, I slither.
I roar through the trees
like the loud rutting howler,
I'm the man-eating cayman
on watch at the runnel.

FLORENTINO
On watch at the runnel.
When nothing comes passing,
smart watchers turn silly.
When nothing comes passing,
I think of a ditty

que me lo enseñó mi abuelo:
"al que me pone la barba
lo raspo de contrapelo".   620
Para pájaro mañoso
munición en el revuelo,
para caimán el arpón
para guabina el anzuelo.
Patiquín que estriba corto
no corre caballo en pelo.
¿Con qué se seca la cara
el que no carga pañuelo?
¿Pá qué se limpia las patas
el que va a dormí en el suelo?   630

Albricias pido, señores

EL DIABLO
El que va a dormí en el suelo
pega en la tierra el oío:
si tiene el sueño liviano
nunca lo matan dormío.
Los gallos están cantando,
escúcheles los cantíos,
los perros están aullando:
recuerde lo convenío.   640
"Zamuros de la Barrosa,
del Alcornocal del Frío
albricias pido, señores
que ya Florentino es mío".

FLORENTINO
Que ya Florentino es mío.
Pacto sin consentimiento
es palabra sin sentío.
¡Néngueres de Banco Seco!
¡taro-taros del Pionío!   650
Présteme no más las alas

46

my grandpappy taught me:
"A man who gives trouble,
I rough him up double."
A bird flying tricky
I shoot as he doubles,
I harpoon the cayman,
I hook the guabina.
A short-stirrup ninny
takes no bareback ride.
if you don't have a hanky
how's a face to be dried?
Why wash your bare feet
if you're sleeping outside?

I give you a toast, sirs!

THE DEVIL
If you're sleeping outside,
your ear's to the ground:
light sleepers avoid
any danger of murder.
The cockerels are crowing,
take note of their sound:
the wild dogs are howling,
recall what you promised!
"Black vultures of Claymire,
of Cold Corkwood Forest!
I give you a toast, sirs!
Florentino is mine."

FLORENTINO
"Florentino is mine."
A deal never struck
is a word with no meaning.
Come, you plovers of Drybank,
you ibis, sharp-tailed!
Just lend me your wings

pa' que no pare el corrío,
que parado ví al inerme.
Si me dice que soy suyo
será que me le he vendío,
si me le vendí me paga,
porque yo a nadie le fío.
Yo no soy rancho veguero   660
que le mete el agua el río,
yo no soy pájaro bobo
pá'estar calentando nío.

EL DIABLO
Pá'estar calentando nío.
No sé si es pájaro bobo
pero va por un tendío
con la fatiga del remo
en el golpe mal medío;
y en la orilla del silencio   670
se le anudará el tañío
cuando yo mande a parar
el trueno y el desafío.

FLORENTINO
El trueno y el desafío.
Yo con el que no conozco
ni me enserio ni me río,
y me tienen sin cuidao
arrestos del presumío,
porque hoy con gloria de ayer   680
no se enraiza poderío.
Barranca en terreno propio
es mejor que hato en baldío
laudo que ordena despojo
libera al comprometío
dígale al que da lo ajeno
que me dé no más lo mío.

so we needn't stop singing:
he's halting, he's failed!
If he says I am his,
then I am the vendor,
if I did, he must pay me,
for I won't be a lender.
You won't catch me farming
flood-plains by the river,
no booby-bird warming
a nest for another.

THE DEVIL
A nest for another.
A booby or no,
you're caught in deep water,
an oarsman exhausted,
untidily sculling:
I'll tie up your top note
on silence's shore,
when I call a halt to
the thunder, the bluster.

FLORENTINO
The thunder, the bluster.
With one I don't know, I
can't joke nor be serious,
no, nor could I care less
for arrogant swagger.
Today grows no power
on yesterday's glory.
Better own a poor gully
than acres of nowhere.
Words warranting plunder
don't bind: who apportions
the goods of another,
let him give me my own, sir.

EL DIABLO
Que me dé no más lo mío.
Lo suyo es deuda probada   690
con un pagaré vencío.
Por eso llegué temprano
y mi deber lo he cumplío:
atropellarle el cansancio
y frenarle el desvarío
como si se fuera yendo
mucho antes de haber venío
pa' que no vuelva a olvidar
ni en invierno ni en estío
que hoy siendo ayer de mañana   700
mañana de ayer ha sío.

FLORENTINO
Mañana de ayer ha sío.
A mí lo mismo me da
tempranero que tardío
que el tarde siempre es temprano
pa' quien canta amanecío.
Me gusta escuchar el rayo
aunque me deje aturdío,
me gusta correr chubasco   710
si el viento lleva tronío.
¡Águila sobre la quema,
reto del toro bravío!
¡Música de los palmares
por donde no anda el gentío!
¡Limpios dedos de la sombra
pulsando al mundo dormío!
Cuando esas voces me llaman
siempre les he respondío.
¡Cómo me puede callar   720
coplero recién vestío,
gastándose una garganta
tan rebuena... pa' un resfrío!

THE DEVIL
Let him give me my own, sir.
Your own's a debt, proven,
an expired IOU.
For this I came promptly,
fulfilled what was due:
I tripped your tired rhyming,
put a stop to your raving.
How soon you'll be leaving!
You've hardly done coming!
Come winter come summer,
today, just remember,
is yesterday's future,
tomorrow's back number.

FLORENTINO
Tomorrow's back number.
To me it's all one
whether early or late
for late is still early
to the earlybird singer.
I love to hear thunder
no less if it stuns me,
to ride in the rainstorm,
wind roaring all round me.
Sand burning, bull's anger,
the flight of the eagle!
The music of palm-groves
all empty of people!
Clean fingers of shadows
that stroke the world's slumber!
I always have heeded
these voices that called.
Can a songster suppress me,
fresh-laundered, crisp-clothed,
who wears out his windpipe
just right... to catch cold!

EL DIABLO
Tan rebuena… pa' un resfrío.
Aunque me llame a la burla
mi rumbo no lo desvío:
mano a mano y pecho a pecho
ando atizándome el brío
con el fuego del romance   730
que es don de mi señorío.
Yo soy quien soplé ceniza
en la mies del labrantío;
y cuando prendí a mi luto
cinta del mal florecío,
ni me olvidé del recuerdo
ni me acordé del olvío.

FLORENTINO
Ni me acordé del olvío.
Orillas del olvidar   740
recorro mis tiempos íos
cuando poblaban cocuyos
las tinieblas del (h)erío,
y en los quebrantos de arena
con sed de cinco sentíos
iba zurciendo chaparros
cordón de luz con rocío.
Hoy me pongo a inventariar
la hacienda que no he vendío:
voluntad que enciende rumbo   750
querencia que apaga hastío,
pensamiento que campea
de sol a sol florecío.
Me queda lo que he enseñao
perdiendo lo que he aprendío.

EL DIABLO
Perdiendo lo que he aprendío.
Me dio el viento su alma errante,

THE DEVIL
Just right... to catch cold!
You may banter and jest
but I keep to my course:
hand to hand, chest to chest
I go stoking my force
with flame of the poem,
the gift of my prowess.
On the fields of the fall
it is I who blow ashes:
I tie my grim ribbon
of evil's foul fruiting,
I forget no recall,
I recall no forgetting.

FLORENTINO
I recall no forgetting.
On oblivion's strand
I relive my time past
when glow-worms pervaded
the shades of the waste,
sand sweltering, burnt,
five senses athirst,
the oaks hitched and threaded
with pinpoints of dew.
Today I take stock
of my unsold estate:
the goad of resolve,
gall solaced by love,
thoughts ranging the field
each morning made new.
What I've taught, I have kept,
what I've learnt, I've forgotten.

THE DEVIL
What I've learnt, I've forgotten.
I've the wind's roving spirit,

la nube su alero umbrío,
su desamparo el desierto   760
la tempestad su alarío.
Relámpagos me alumbraron
desde el horizonte ardío
nariceando cimarrones
y sangrando a los rendíos
con la punta'e mi puñal
que duele y da escalofrío.

FLORENTINO
Que duele y da escalofrío...
Dame campo, pensamiento,   770
y dame rienda, albedrío,
pá'enseñarle al que no sabe
y nunca lo ha comprendío
cuánto espacio inmenso cabe
sobre una frente tendío.
Cimarrones hay que verlos,
de bueyes no le porfío;
escalofríos son miedo,
miedo nunca lo he sentío,
puñal, sáquelo si quiere   780
a ver si repongo el mío.
Duele lo que se perdió
cuando no se ha defendío.

EL DIABLO
Cuando no se ha defendío
lo que se perdió no importa
si está de pies el vencío,
de pies sobre la atalaya
del pecho entenebrecío
porque el orgullo indomable   790
vale más que el bien perdío.
Por eso a usted me lo llevo
centellas por atavío,

the clouds are my awning,
I've despair from the desert,
the storm-cry's my warning.
I'm lit up by lightning
from burning horizons,
I pierce wild bulls' noses,
draw blood from the broken:
at the point of my blade
they are shivering, shaken.

FLORENTINO
They are shivering, shaken…
Give me space, give me thought,
give me rein, give me freedom
to teach the untutored
who's not comprehended
how vast is the space
that fits in a forehead.
Wild bulls, a quick glance,
I'll not discuss cattle:
it's fear makes them tremble,
I've never been fearful.
Draw your blade if you choose,
see if mine is upended.
It's grievous to lose
what you've never defended.

THE DEVIL
What you've never defended.
The loss has no meaning
if the loser's still standing
high up on his tower,
his heart plunged in shadow:
for pride undefeated
outweighs lost possession.
And so I shall take you,
all coated with burning,

en bongo de veinte varas
que tiene un golpe sombrío
más profundo y más amargo
que ayes del viento y del río:
rumbo y destino la nada,
pura pena por avío
en la negra madrugada,   800
lejano el amanecer,
se le olvidó a Florentino
la copla del terraplén.

Emboscada

FLORENTINO
La copla del terraplén.
Bordones del alma realenga
la engarzan hoy como ayer
a las tonadas de Apure
y a este golpe barinés   810
que lo silban los turpiales
en la boca del Pagüey.

EL DIABLO
En la boca del Pagüey
les entro a los remolinos
con el timón al revés,
y al rompe sé si el aguaje
es de tronco o es de pez.
Por las vueltas y los chorros
llevo el bongo sin vaivén.   820

FLORENTINO
Llevo el bongo sin vaivén.
Así la leyenda cruzan
cantares de buena ley
romance de mil caminos
rosal del marchito pie:

in a sixty-foot skiff,
grim rhythm its driver,
wailing deeper, more bitter
than wild wind and river,
bound away into nothing:
pure pain for your garment
before the black dawning:
far off from the morning,
Florentino forgetting
the plains and the singing.

Ambush

FLORENTINO
The plains and the singing.
Free souls have harp-rhythm,
Barinas still strumming,
with tunes from the river
Apure, for ever:
the troupials trill them
at the mouth of Pagüey.

THE DEVIL
At the mouth of Pagüey
I enter fierce eddies,
reversing my tiller:
I know from the wake
what's athwart, fish or timber.
Through twisting white water
I hold the boat steady.

FLORENTINO
I hold the boat steady.
So legend reposes
in gallant old songs
and well-travelled stories
and doddering roses.

¡Como perfuma los siglos
tu rosa sin marchitez!

EL DIABLO
Tu rosa sin marchitez   830
la encarna en color y espina
quien la pinta sin pincel;
por fin le escucho palabra
que la siento yo también
cuando siento la dolida
tentación de florecer.

FLORENTINO
Tentación de florecer.
El jazmín del espinito
besó la tierra y se fue,   840
desde la salida de aguas
hasta que empezó a llover,
cuando puntea el rocío
el pasaje del clavel.

EL DIABLO
El pasaje del clavel.
Esa música no se oye
donde el verde no se ve:
las garúas cristalinas
son sólo para el vergel;   850
para el yermo y los pesares,
soplo de impávida sed.

FLORENTINO
Soplo de impávida sed
arranca fresco susurro
al palmar de mi caney
donde la tierra callada
va de merced en merced

Sweet scent down the ages,
your rose ever young!

THE DEVIL
Your rose ever young.
He who paints with no brush
paints its colour and thorn.
At last you have spoken
as I feel in my bosom:
I ache with temptation,
with craving to blossom.

FLORENTINO
With craving to blossom.
The jasmine kissed earth
as it fell from the thorn,
when the waters withdrew,
till the fresh falls of rain
set in pinpoints of dew
the carnation again.

THE DEVIL
The carnation again.
In the place never green,
such music's not heard.
The lightness of rain,
only orchards deserve:
through the wasteland of pain,
thirst blows undeterred.

FLORENTINO
Thirst blows undeterred:
but a breeze whispers cool
in the palms by my cabin,
where earth sunk in silence
finds mercies abundant,

de la pata del samán
a la orilla del jagüey: 860
palo que supo florear
pozo soñando correr.

EL DIABLO
Pozo soñando correr.
No le envidio al agua inmóvil
su marchita limpidez,
de dos en dos sus yaguasos
sus garzas de cien en cien,
desamparada su luna,
pensativa su mudez   870
desierto de los verdores
sin vacada ni corcel.

FLORENTINO
Sin vacada ni corcel
mi rumbo no me lo cambian
presagios de mercader
yo camino con la estrella
lirio de luz y de fe
aliento de eternidad
aspiran los que la ven.   880

EL DIABLO
Aspiran los que la ven
cuando va dejando al irse
servidumbre de volver,
penitencia de alumbrar
sin saber dónde ni a quién.
La eternidad es de todos
como el odiar y el querer,
tan sombra como la vida,
tan dolor como el laurel.   890

from the trunk of samán
to the brink of the pool:
a tree versed in blooming,
pond dreaming of streaming.

THE DEVIL
Pond dreaming of streaming.
I don't envy water
its moribund stillness,
its ducks in their couples,
its herons in hundreds,
its moonlight defenceless,
its ominous silence,
no plants fresh and verdant,
no cattle, no horse.

FLORENTINO
No cattle, no horse.
On forecasts of traders
I don't change my course.
I follow the star,
the lily, the faith:
eternity's breath
they breathe, who can see it.

THE DEVIL
They breathe, who can see it
depart in subjection,
obliged to return
in penance to lighten
some place or some person.
Eternity's common,
like hating and loving:
as sombre as living,
pain bitter as laurel.

FLORENTINO
Tan dolor como el laurel
dolor dan copas desnudas
si matan su verdecer,
mas no la que alzan en mayo
bucare y araguaney:
defendiendo lo que toco
lucho por lo que soñé.
Andante de mi destino
por serle fiel a lo fiel,   900
en brasero de lo humilde
ví la luz de la altivez.

EL DIABLO
Ví la luz de la altivez.
Rozador de la amargura
taló el fondo de mi ser.
Mi sino es quitar si vieron
y dar, cuando nadie dé,
ceniza en la llamarada,
brasas en la palidez.   910
Por mí espigan en suspiro
el olvido y el desdén
y aduermen la frente amante
cojines que eternicé.

FLORENTINO
Cojines que eternicé.
Reniego de esos alardes
que no me importa saber.
Razón despierta a las cinco
belleza a golpe de seis   920
cuando bendicen la vida
en la majada la grey
y en la cumbrera del rancho
la seña azul del café.

FLORENTINO
Pain bitter as laurel.
There's pain in bare treetops
whose green died away,
not the May-time bucare
nor araguaney.
I fight for my dreams,
I defend what I hold:
to what's loyal I'm loyal,
I walk my own road,
in the hearth of the humble
see great light of pride.

THE DEVIL
See great light of pride.
The harrow of hurt
cut me down at the root.
What you see, I remove,
what's unsought, I provide:
I pile ash on the blaze,
hot coals on the pallor.
For the proudly oblivious,
I ripen lamenting:
my pillows lull lovers
to sleep never-ending.

FLORENTINO
To sleep never-ending.
I spurn your vain show,
I don't wish to know.
At five, reason's woken,
at six, beauty's roused:
life's blessing is spoken
by herd safely housed
and smoke-wisp ascending,
the coffee's blue token.

EL DIABLO
La seña azul del café.
Ay, catire Florentino,
trovador del terraplén,
que soñó quitar pesares
y le quitaron la fe,   930
que quiso ser toro altivo
y lo enyugan como al buey
apréndase desde ahora
lo que le falta saber:
que bajo el cielo marchito
tan sólo el oro y la miel
alivian para el quien sabe
el suspiro del tal vez.

FLORENTINO
El suspiro del tal vez.   940
Esas nubes no hacen sombra
si camina por sus pies
el que nunca cuenta males
porque contó con su bien,
y el mejor cuento lo guarda
para contárselo a usté,
cuando descorra sus lutos
la noche de Santa Inés
y el alba prenda una rosa
en el ojal del jagüey.   950

EL DIABLO
En el ojal del jagüey
al vislumbrar su facundia
predije su impavidez
de corsario entre los bravos
marinos de mi bajel:
varón para buen comando,
buen vino y buena mujer,

THE DEVIL
The coffee's blue token.
Fair-face Florentino!
You bard of broad plains,
who thought to soothe sorrows,
your faith has been broken!
You would-be proud bull
now yoked like a bullock,
take note of this lesson,
you need to be told:
under lack-lustre heaven
it's by honey and gold
alone, that some person,
some pain is consoled.

FLORENTINO
Some pain is consoled.
These clouds cast no chill
if on two feet one goes,
not reckoning woes:
recounts his goodwill,
and keeps his best tale
for telling to you,
when at Santa Inés
night's curtains recoil,
and dawn pins a rose
on the breast of the pool.

THE DEVIL
On the breast of the pool
I noticed your skill,
I knew you'd be fearless,
a corsair, around
my vessel's brave sailors:
a man of command,
good wine, a good woman:

porque el destino le puso
lauro de abismo en la sien.   960

FLORENTINO
Lauro de abismo en la sien.
de noche cuando transito
plegarias de mi niñez,
vuelan las avemarías
con la garza del amén,
"por si me quieren tentar
el que hace la cruz en el agua
para poderla beber."

EL DIABLO   970
Para poderla beber.
A ese pájaro mendigo
ojalá nada le den
como a mí que los maizales
le abran mazorca sin mies;
como yo que siento el río
y nunca me sacié en él.
Siguiendo el trazo del humo
que como azogue lo atrajo,
le salgo por otro rumbo   980
a ver si topa el atajo.

Ahora verán, señores

FLORENTINO
A ver si topa el atajo.
Si registró el clarinete,
no me toque el contrabajo
ni me suene esos platillos
como carreta en cascajo,
que todo renglón no es verso
ni rima con conchas de ajo,   990

66

by fate you are crowned
with the laurel of failures.

FLORENTINO
With the laurel of failures.
At night when I say
my old childhood prayers,
up fly the Hail Marys
with heron's amen,
"to thwart one who traces
the cross on the water,
and thirsts until then."

THE DEVIL
And thirsts until then.
That bird who goes begging,
I hope it gets nothing,
like me when the maize
gives me cobs without corn:
like me at the river,
no draught ever drawn.
I swerve with the smoke
like tinsel of tinning,
I take a new track,
can you go where I'm turning?

Now sirs, you will see

FLORENTINO
Can you go where I'm turning?
If you chose clarinet, sir
don't give me bassooning,
don't clank your brass platters
like an ox-cart's rough running:
some rhymes are not coming
when garlic needs skinning,

ni el secreto del repique
es guindarse del badajo.
El arte es hasta en el cielo
disciplina sin relajo
si un arcángel desafina
ya el director se distrajo.

EL DIABLO
Ya el director se distrajo
pensando en los humoristas
de escofina y estropajo   1000
que a quien la cara bajó
lo apodan "escarabajo",
al vizconde "conde bizco"
y "amarra ajos" al marrajo.
De esos necios pergaminos
yo arrugué más de un legajo
aunque me vista de nuevo
respeto el ajeno andrajo:
cuando canto con un hombre
con el grito lo encorajo,   1010
con la audacia lo sacudo,
con el numen lo aventajo;
lo venzo y no lo abochorno
lo castigo y no lo ultrajo.

FLORENTINO
Lo castigo y no lo ultrajo
yo en refriegas no torturo,
pero tampoco agasajo:
si no le echo plomo al tigre
me come el tigre en atajo,   1020
y cuando no haya un becerro
me atropella el zarandajo.
Si usted es quien me atosiga
con mil golpes a destajo,
¡que culpa voy yo a tener

bell-clappers aren't happy
when ringers hang clowning.
Art, even in heaven,
is all disciplining:
archangels sing flat, when
conductor's gone swanning.

THE DEVIL
Conductor's gone swanning:
'File a hoof, love a loofah!'
—he's musing on punning.
For the downbeat, despondent,
Dung-Beetle's his kenning:
the Viscount's an '*Eye-Squint*',
'*trapscallions*' the cunning.
I've crumpled thick parchments
of legal unmeaning,
I'm spruce, yet respect
others' patching and darning.
When I sing with a man, my
top note sets him churning,
by boldness I shake him,
by wizardry winning:
I crush but don't shame him,
I trounce without spurning.

FLORENTINO
I trounce without spurning.
I shun chinese burning,
not whining nor fawning.
If I don't shoot the tiger
he'll eat me, no warning:
no calf in the offing,
I'm bushmeat for dining.
Sir, if you molest me
with summary dunning,
what good to protest

si en el retrueque lo rajo!
Contraje mi obligación,
la misma que usted contrajo:
fajármele frente a frente,
frente a frente me le fajo.   1030
"Zamuros de la Barrosa
de Arcornocal de abajo,
les presento al pesador
que nunca saló el tasajo.
Ahora verán, señores,
al Diablo pasar trabajo."

EL DIABLO
Al Diablo pasar trabajo.
No miente al que no conoce
ni finja ese desparpajo,   1040
haciéndose el que no duele
el filo con que lo sajo
mire que por esta tierra
no es primera vez que viajo,
y aquí saben los señores
que si las uñas encajo
lo disperso lo reúno
lo entero lo desmigajo,
lo cuajado lo derrito,
lo derretido lo cuajo,   1050
al mismo limón chiquito
me lo chupo gajo a gajo.

FLORENTINO
Me lo chupo gajo a gajo.
Usté que se alza el copete
y yo que se lo rebajo.
No se asusten, compañeros,
déjenlo, que yo lo atajo,
déjenlo que suelte el bongo
pá que le coja agua abajo;   1060

if my backlash is stunning!
I signed on the line,
the same as your signing,
to tussle head on:
head on I'm sustaining.
"Black vultures of Claymire,
of Corkwoods Deep Downing,
meet the cheat, the purveyor
of beef that wants brining.
Now sirs, you shall see
The Evil One straining."

THE DEVIL
The Evil One straining:
don't fib, you don't know me.
Don't fake your buffooning
as I carve with my blade:
no pretence of no paining!
This land I have learned
by frequent returning:
these gentlemen know
my sharp nails' campaigning,
dispersing the gathered,
the scattered convening:
dissolving the clotted
I clot the free-running.
I suck little limes,
every bitter bit draining.

FLORENTINO
Every bitter bit draining.
You raise your crest high
which I soon shall be downing.
No worries, my friends,
he's mine for the pruning.
Let him be! in his boat,
for raining, or drowning,

déjenlo parar rodeo
que yo se lo desparpajo,
déjenlo que pinte suertes
yo sabré si le barajo.
Déjenlo encajar las uñas
que yo me las desencajo.
Déjenlo alzar la cabeza,
que va a salir cabizbajo
antes que Dios amanezca
se lo lleva quien lo trajo 1070
alante el caballo fino,
atrás el burro marrajo.
¡Quién ha visto dorodoro
cantando con arrendajo!
Cuando talla briscas de oro
el madrugador fanal
si me cambió el consonante
yo se lo puedo cambiar.

Ecos lejanos repiten

EL DIABLO 1080
Yo se lo puedo cambiar.
Los graves y los agudos
a mí lo mismo me dan:
lo mismo son en tiniebla
muchedumbre y soledad
a quien dejó lo infalible
soñando luz del quizá
a quien la paz sin la gloria
cambió por gloria sin paz,
que mucho es rimar querella 1090
con el nunca o el jamás.

FLORENTINO
Con el nunca o el jamás.
Su aguijón no me zahiere

let him set up his show,
which I'll be detuning,
let him hope for good cards,
I'll be dealing and dunning.
Let him dig in his claws,
I'll unfasten his pinning:
let him raise up his head,
he shall slink out resigning,
One who brought him shall lead
before God's own good morning:
he'll trail the fine steed
like an ass of low cunning.
Can a vulture compete
with a Chieftain's fine tuning?
When the great lantern forms
gold twists at day's coming,
if he altered my rhymes,
I can alter his rhyming.

Distant echoes repeat

THE DEVIL
I can alter his rhyming.
The high notes, the low notes,
to me it's all one:
all one in my darkness
the crowds, the alone:
for a bright dream of Maybe
I left certain safety,
quit inglorious peace
for an unpeaceful glory:
it's hard to rhyme grudging
with Never and Nothing.

FLORENTINO
With Never and Nothing.
Your barb does not wound me,

ni me emponzoña su mal
ni en escombros de deshecho
me arredra su adversidad
porque este pasaje suyo
es como el del gavilán
que aguaitando la perdiz   1100
se topó al águila real.
Y en el pleito que tuvieron
el águila pudo más
con el pico que le puso
el que le dio majestad
y las alas invencibles
de quien la enseñó a volar.

EL DIABLO
De quien le enseño a volar.
¡Ay!, catire Florentino,   1110
cantor de pecho cabal.
¡Que tenebroso el camino
que nunca desandará
por negra orilla del mundo
donde ni suspiros hay
ni vuela la corocora
ni susurra la torcaz.
Sin alero ni rescoldo
sin luna ni morichal
sin alante sin arriba,   1120
sin orilla y sin atrás,
donde olvida patria y nombre
el que ya no puede hablar.

FLORENTINO
El que ya no puede hablar.
A nadie le ando escondiendo
mi estatuto personal
mis bienes son lo que doy
y mi nombre el que me dan

your poison, your evil:
your hate does not scare me,
reduce me to rubble.
Your song's like the hawk's
who hunted the partridge
and met with the king,
the great golden eagle:
and when they contended,
the eagle prevailed
with the beak that One gave him
who rendered him regal,
the invincible wings
he received to go soaring.

THE DEVIL
He received to go soaring.
Florentino, fair face,
you great-hearted singer!
How dismal the trail
you'll never retrace,
black brink of the world
a place of no sighing,
no soaring red ibis,
no whispering dove.
No eaves and no embers,
no palm-grove, no moon,
no forward, no upward,
no backward, no bourn:
lost name and lost country,
a speechless forgetting.

FLORENTINO
A speechless forgetting.
I never dissemble
my personal standing:
what I have's what I give
and my name is as given,

domiciliado en mi huella 1130
soltero y mayor de edad.
Cuatro alumbradas de cielo
alinderan mi heredad
y une la manga del viento
al oriente con mi alar.
Mi cruz son el horizonte
y el rumbo de mi alazán,
mis expedientes las nubes
mi archivo la inmensidad;
mi renta silbo y tonada 1140
caminos mi capital:
pagué los que anduve y debo
los que quedan por andar.

EL DIABLO
Los que quedan por andar
le toca trocharlos hoy
con mi rejo en el bozal,
por la ley que dio a la arena
el rumbo del huracán.
¡Ay!, catire Florentino, 1150
trovero del chaparral,
¿qué vale no querer irse
en voz de quien ya se va?
¿Qué delito hay en la espina?
¿Qué son en la nada lóbrega
verso y música fugaz,
sino esperanza que solas
se desesperanzarán?
¿Qué son flechas del amor
en la irredenta ansiedad, 1160
sino burlescas y tristes
carcajadas del carcaj?
Ya no valen su baquía,
su fe ni su facultá,
catire quita pesares,

my home's where I travel,
I'm adult and single.
My estate is marked out
by four lanterns in heaven,
the wind with its sleeves
joins the east to my eaves.
My cross, my horse heading
towards the horizon:
the clouds keep my papers,
the vastness my files:
my rents are the rhyming,
my wealth is the trails.
I've paid where I've passed:
where I'm going, I'm owing.

THE DEVIL
Where I'm going I'm owing.
You'll blaze trails today,
you're bridled for towing:
like sand in the sway
of the storm, you'll obey.
Fair-face Florentino,
the greenwood trouvère,
why say you're unwilling?
you're now halfway there.
Don't blame me for needling!
In the dolorous void
what are music and word
but hopes disappearing
in total despair?
What are Eros' arrows
when terror's for ever,
but mockeries, sorrows
discharged from the quiver?
No use your acumen,
your faith and your skill,
you lily-faced sunbeam,

arrendajo y turupial.
Tahúres en mi tapete
tiran sena y ¡siempre el as!
Rebeldes hacia mi sombra
no quieren y ¡siempre van!   1170

FLORENTINO
No quieren y siempre van.
De andar solo esa vereda
los pies se le han de secar,
y se le hará más profunda
la mala arruga en la faz,
porque mientras llano y cielo
me den de luz su caudal,
mientras la voz se me escuche
por sobre la tempestá,   1180
yo soy quien marco mi rumbo
con el timón del cantar.
Y si al dicho pido ayuda
aplíquese esta verdá:
que no manda marinero
donde manda capitán.

EL DIABLO
Donde manda capitán
usted es vela caída,
yo altivo son de la mar.   1190
Ceniza será su voz,
rescoldo de muerto afán,
sed será su última huella,
náufraga en el arenal;
humo serán sus caminos,
piedra sus sueños serán,
carbón será su recuerdo,
lo negro en la eternidad.
Para que no me responda
ni se me resista más,   1200

proud songbird, troupial.
The cheats at my baize
throw a six, then a one!
Resisting my shades
they protest, they are gone!

FLORENTINO
They protest, they are gone!
You'll be walking alone,
dry feet on poor footing,
on your face even deeper
that horrible scar.
Light comes to me, flooding
from sky and from plain:
my voice is still heard in
the roar of the rain.
I mark out my heading,
my helm's the refrain:
this saying will aid me,
this truth will obtain:
Jack Tar gives no orders
where the Captain commands.

THE DEVIL
Where the Captain commands
you're a tumbledown sail,
I'm the sea's mighty roar.
Your voice will be ashes,
dead embers of toil,
and thirst your last vestige,
washed up on the shore:
your trails will be smoke,
your dreams will be stone,
your memory cinders,
black, black evermore.
You'll make no reply,
you'll resist me no more,

Capitán de la Tiniebla
es quien lo viene a buscar.

FLORENTINO
Es quien lo viene a buscar.
Mucho gusto en conocerlo
tengo, señor Satanás.
Zamuros de la Barrosa,
salgan del Alcornocal,
tíñanse las alas negras
con lebruna claridá,   1210
de esa que mana el Oriente
cuando se vuelve el rosal,
que al Diablo lo cogió el día
queriéndome atropellar
y le falló la malicia
con el último compás.

EL DIABLO
Con el último compás
ni el arte le dará escudo
ni rezos lo salvarán.   1220
Vampiros sobre la frente
—vivo y lóbrego antifaz—
el presagio del abismo
en el luto del callar,
ya lo aguarda el centinela
de la "Doliente Ciudá".
Mire sus señas sombrías
en el fúnebre portal.

FLORENTINO
En el fúnebre portal   1230
lindero de su garita
quédese con su guardián,
que la ley no da tutela
no habiendo minoridá,

The Captain of Darkness
will get you for sure.

FLORENTINO
Will get you for sure.
My pleasure to know you,
Mr Satan, for sure.
Black vultures of Claymire,
come fly from the Corkwoods
and tint your black wings
with this pale golden ray:
by the streaming of day
from the east, like a rose,
Old Nick has been caught!
He tried hard to trip me:
his malice fell short
in the very last measure.

THE DEVIL
In the very last measure
no art will protect you,
no prayers will save you.
Your brow black with vampires
—a grim living mask—
forewarns of the chasm
of muteness and pain
in the Suffering City:
the sentry is there:
see the signals of dusk
at the gates of despair.

FLORENTINO
At the gates of despair,
the bounds of your gaming,
you'll halt with your warder,
for the law takes no care,
since I am no minor:

y yo soy el ruletero
de mi envite y de mi azar.
Le abrí parada al destino
pero no perdí jamás
ni el clavel del arrebol
ni el tapiz del arenal,   1240
ni del mantel de mi mesa
el limpio don de mi pan:
porque regué con sudores
la siembra del buen soñar;
y si caminé de noche
sé que vale mucho más
un segundo de lucero
que siglos de oscuridá.

EL DIABLO
Que siglos de oscuridá.   1250
Los remolinos del río
ya suenan bajo su alar:
antes que el agua le llegue,
suspire el adiós fatal.
Despídase de la luz
y medite al suspirar:
si gime el mal en tiniebla,
¿quién alumbra la maldá?
Despídase del amor
y pregunte al suspirar: 1260
en cordajes del ensueño,
¿quién templa el bordón del ¡ay!?
Despídase de la fe
y medite al suspirar:
¿qué delito es la mentira
si lo triste es la verdá?
Despídase de las horas
y recuerde al suspirar
que a quien penó por lo eterno
penas lo eternizarán.   1270

I play my roulette,
I place bets at hazard.
My stakes were at risk
yet I never have squandered
the sunset's carnation,
the sandbank's close pattern,
the cloth of my table,
clean gift of my bread:
with sweat I have watered
the crop of good dreaming.
At night if I'm roaming,
I know there's more value
in a second of starlight
than in ages of shadow.

THE DEVIL

Than in ages of shadow.
The river sends eddies
right under your roof,
the waters are closing:
sigh death's last farewell!
Goodbye to the light,
take thought as you sigh:
malice groans in the murk,
who lights the dread dark?
Take leave of your love
reflect as you sigh:
on your harp of delusion,
who sounds the deep cry?
Take leave of your faith,
take thought as you sigh:
if sorrow's the truth,
is it evil to lie?
Take leave of the hours
recall as you sigh:
he who strove to endure
shall have strife evermore.

Despídase de la cruz
y no piense al suspirar.

FLORENTINO
Y no piense al suspirar.
Sácame de esto con Dios
Virgen de la Soledá,
Virgen del Carmen bendita,
sagrada Virgen del Real,
tierna Virgen del Socorro,
dulce Virgen de la Paz,   1280
serena Virgen de Lourdes
con tu fuente por altar,
Virgen de la Coromoto,
Virgen de Chiquinquirá,
señora de la corteza
que en cedro esculpes tu faz
piadosa Virgen del Valle,
santa Virgen del Pilar,
Virgen de piedra admirable,
patrona del manantial,   1290
Fiel Madre de los Dolores
dame el fulgor que tú das.
¡San Miguel! dame tu escudo,
tu rejón y tu puñal,
Niño de Atocha bendito,
Santísima Trinidá.
(En compases de silencio
negro bongo que echa a andar.
¡Salud, señores! El alba
bebiendo en el paso real).   1300
Ecos lejanos repiten:
Santísima Trinidá.

Take leave of the cross,
never think of the sigh.

FLORENTINO
Never think of the sigh.
Come save me, Our Lady
of Solitude, Lady
of Carmel, Blest Lady
of El Real, Lady
of Succour, Sweet Lady
of Peace, Serene Lady
of Lourdes, your fountain
for an altar, Our Lady
of Coromoto, Our Lady
of Chiquinquirá,
your face carved in cedar's
rough bark—Pious Lady
of the Vale, Saintly Lady
of the Pillar—stone miracle,
stream's Holy Patron—
with God's aid, Our Lady,
faithful Mother of Sorrows,
grant me your bright splendour!
your shield and your sword,
St Michael, defender!
Blest Child of Atocha!
O Most Holy Trinity!
(The music has ceased,
the black boat departs.
Sirs, your health! The dawn drinks
in the Pass of the King.)
Distant echoes repeat:
O most holy Trinity!

NOTES

The very full notes up to about line 300 are by Gloria Carnevali, setting the scene; the remainder by Timothy Adès are written with her guidance.

El Contrapunteo de Florentino y el Diablo is one of the most popular poems from *Los Llanos*, the Plains of Venezuela. The legend goes that Florentino was the epitome of the great *llanero*: handsome, a great rider and cattleman, a ladies' man, but above all, a singer and poet. His improvisations (*corríos, contrapunteos*) were so fast and to the point that the Devil got jealous and challenged him to a night of singing. If the Devil wins before dawn, Florentino will go back with him to Hell. Florentino's prize is simply to have defeated the Devil.

There are sixteen types of *joropo*, and fifty-eight variations, available to accompany this music. Cattlemen improvise every evening, as they settle for a song before going to bed...

1-4 *El coplero* is the singer of *coplas*. As in flamenco, these are rhymed songs, most often improvised. Florentino is immediately identified as a poet-singer: he is famous for it.

El Desamparo is a place with an ominous name which suggests the vulnerability of Florentino to the advances of the Devil. (The ranch of the famously wicked Doña Bárbara was called *El Miedo*, Fear). If you have no *amparo*, you have no shelter, no protection. He is evidently coming from the Desamparo as he is retracing his steps, *desanda el camino*. *A golpe de seis:* on the chime of a bell at six o'clock. *El ancho terraplén* suggests that this is the dry period in the Llanos (six months of rain and six months of dry season); that the land, flooded at times, is now totally dry, which is why the *terraplén*, a flat and hard extent of *tierra*, is so wide, *ancho*. So here we have a singer-poet at dusk on the dry Llanos, coming from a menacing place.

5-8 He is alone with his horse, and perhaps also lonely. Seasonal fires have made the scene black and desolate, matching his mood.

Florentino was a lover: he may have dramatic memories, *llamas de ayer*, flames of yesterday... His mount is a *corcel*, a fine old word for horse. The horse's hooves stir up the loose soil, *tierra errante*, raising a *macolla*, a sort of dust cloud, as he moves...

13-22 *Los escuálidos espinos desnudan su amarillez:* the land is drying out, yellow and grey with brittle plants and dust. As the heat rises, the water-holes are the only places where animals and plants find some life. They shrink, and the animals, whether cattle or wild, either migrate or die; the plants wither away. *Chicharras* are a kind of very loud cricket, with a deafening, infuriating song. They usually sing in moments of great heat, and if they are singing at sunset, it means that this is the driest moment of the season, when everything is *ceniciento,* ashen: *cenizo anochecer.* In the wet season, the *moriche* palms sway in the wind. When the weather is about to change, the wind announces the rain and everything is set in motion. At such a time, to see the mottled surface of the water, the flight of the birds, is pure telluric magic. But Florentino is riding just before this happens, the atmosphere is so deadly calm that the stillness of the palm, *sin un vaivén*, signals the stillness of the whole world, *parece que para el mundo.* He, a lonely poet, is oblivious of this, and rides on this rough patch of earth, *erial*, as if he were in a green cultivated land, a *vergel.* The *vive su grave altivez* stresses the inward-looking, proudly dismissive, stoic attitude of Florentino toward the perils and discomforts of the world. He has to be like that to accept hell as his possible fate, so soon after.

23-41 A *caño* is a branch of water emerging from a main stream. It may not actually flow: it can become a pool, *jagüey*, sometimes enormous, but it is not a spring. Florentino is dying of thirst: *estoy muerto de sed.* ...We see this as if we were Florentino himself. So far, we have seen him from afar but the poetic eye draws the camera in. He knows the water is clear because he can see in the *jagüey* the forelegs of his chestnut horse. The horse becomes an important point of reference for the chilling phenomenon that will happen. Descriptions of sight, touch and sound vie to make it even more uncanny. *El cacho* is a hollowed cowhorn used by the *llaneros* as a water container, and carried *en bandolière*, maybe, certainly with a string attached so that they can throw and retrieve it from the water without dismounting. Florentino throws it once and knows it has hit the water because first he hears it and then drops of water wet his feet, *salpican*. Florentino would not be bare-footed, he may have worn *alpargatas*, a kind of espadrilles made of leather, or most probably boots. It is not clear whether the *salpicado* is perceived as a wet sensation on the skin or as the sight of wet marks on his feet. Yet the horn reaches his lips empty. He throws it down again and this time, the *cacho* makes a splash in the water, another use of *salpica*. We are not told how he knows this, he may have both seen and heard the splash. The next thing he hears is a whispering sound, *sorbo*, from his avid horse's underlip. P*alafrén* is another very old-fashioned word for horse. Much of the *llaneros'* vocabulary comes from poetry contests held in *el Siglo de Oro* in Spain: the 16th-century Golden Age. The people, hearing or reading these poems, would learn them by heart and, little by little, incorporate similes, metaphors and vocabulary into their own sung poetry contests. As Florentino draws the *cacho* up for the second time, a rosary of droplets hangs from the string: another visual sign of the presence of water, but all *he* sees is sand at the murky bottom of it. The rosary is called *dulce*: we are in a Catholic country.

42-75 *Soplo de quema el suspiro*: Florentino is denied water and sighs; his sigh is as hot as the wind that blows through a fire. We go back to the *quema* theme, the burning of the vegetation by campesinos and the indigenous people to clear the land. As there is no water, the ear of a cereal or of corn is drooping, empty, *sin mies* (barley or oats: there is little or no wheat in Venezuela). The next two lines are like a hallucination: burning sap *savia ardiendo en la imagen de nunca reverdecer*, stops Forentino, or the reader, from believing that the world will ever be green again. In this rather hopeless mood, Florentino decides to call it a day, longingly looks towards his home, *caney*, and heads in that direction. As he is doing so, he hears a 'sombre' trot behind him: someone is following him, suddenly, out of nowhere. The rider comes into sight, though not entirely, because it is already dark and he is in black. Florentino distinguishes a black *manta*, a sort of poncho, a black horse and a black felt hat which looks like velvet. The *guama* is a flat, stiff pod with a furry lining, up to 50cm by 4cm, the seeds having sweet white edible coats. The hat, *el sombrero pelo 'e guama,* is inseparable from a *llanero*. They don't like women touching their hats and there is a famous line, *Sobre mi caballo, yo, sobre mí, mi sombrero, y sobre mi sombrero, Dios.* ('Above my horse, myself...') The three ítems, poncho, hat and horse, identify the rider as a *llanero*. His face is hidden under the deep shadow cast by the hat (which has the shape of a Stetson), so Florentino doesn't see it. But he hears him sing...

The Devil identifies himself as the one who sees everything without having to look, *aquel que ve sin mirar*. True to the *contrapunteo* tradition, he puts his rival on the wrong foot by implying that Florentino doesn't see even if he looks, *aquel que mira sin ver*. These words of his are in high romantic style, which may imply a slower rhythm of delivery. Later they both try to trick each other by changing the rhythm of the *joropo* and therefore of the rhyme.

The word *negro*, black, has now stuck to the Devil, but not in a racial sense. His aesthetics are slightly gothic. He will stage the challenge at *la negra orilla del mundo*. Why does the Devil bother to challenge a mortal? Because he has found his equal in Florentino's poetry: *se han de hallar, se han de encontrar, de quien a quien*, a wonderful formula of equality in which the *quien*, a pronoun, stands for all a person is. They are two contenders of the same weight: and one must outweigh the other. *El río:* sinister characters in Venezuelan imagery always come in a *bongo* or dug-out canoe from the river, which is often identified with eternity. *lo voy a buscar para cantar con usté:* in the singing *buscar* means to reach that point of cleverness where the other cannot reply, *el que me busca me encuentra*, they say: he who comes for me, finds me. *Buscar y cantar* have a tight connection. Santa Inés is evidently a place where people gather to sing in that empty immensity. But if Florentino is the greatest, why should he bother with this challenger? The challenger shows his pedigree: *soy retador de juglares* (jesters must have sung, the jester's wit was difficult to defeat) *desde los siglos del rey...* I am timeless. And then the sting at the end: *Le sobra con esperarme...* all you have to do is wait for me, a very dismissive expression. After the challenge comes a spooky description of the effect the devil has on the place, which Florentino seems not to see, like someone who indeed *mira sin ver*. He is immersed in his musings which arise from his identification with the savannah and from his deep 'post-colonial' condition: he is a Spaniard by origin but an American by fate. He has inherited a language and a faith from his ancestors, but the power of the Llanos is also in him. The settlers who came to Venezuela were mainly from Andalusia: from Seville, Granada and Córdoba. The Andalusians brought all their wonderful music from Al-Andalus from which the *joropo* and the sung poetry derive.

67-98 *Mala sombra del espanto*: in *los Llanos* they enjoy stories of *espantos y aparecidos*. The Llanos have their share of ghosts, erring souls, bad spirits that often strike and kill the living. An *espanto* is someone not quite real, so this character is not just a gothic *llanero*, but someone who has already crossed to the other world. No *espanto* is nice. This one has a body, temporarily at least, for he projects a shadow across the *terraplén*. *Ocaso*: sunset in los llanos can be spectacular, layers of clouds of different colours and luminosity, like streaks of marble. *Mala sombra* is said of a person of ill omen.

Pajas del anochecer: Straws of nightfall cover the shadow and erase it. The shadows of stalks, palms, anything vertical will turn into dark long straws, hiding the Devil and his riders.

76-77 *Coge el banco de través*: he goes off at an angle, changing direction, or keeping his distance.

78-98 He is a man between two cultures, stretching the true tone, *el tono fiel*, like a harpstring between Andalusian America and Spanish Barinas. Barinas is Arvelo's birthplace and Florentino's home State. He is a Barinés and a Spaniard at the same time, so his verse is taut between two continents. In it he lays out the contradictions of the savannah: it is hard toil but you love it, it has so many directions *rumbos,* being so open and yet so still, is full of water yet dying of thirst. The savannah is like him, lonesome or solitary, but he sees God in it. Florentino is a Catholic, a strong believer and he takes the savannah, nature's naked breast, as the base-point of his reply.

100-120 *Joropo* is music of the people, *el pueblo llano. Rancho* is not a ranch, but a house made of *bahareque* (mud and bitter cane) with a thatched roof. This way of building is typical of the area, cheap, ecological and cool. When a man decides to settle down with a woman, he will build a cane structure to the size they want and then cover the walls with a mixture of mud and grass. Thus even farmhands have ample dwellings for singing and dancing. They refer to their homes as *caney* or *rancho.* A *llanero rancho* is one step up, a more complex dwelling, with different rooms, backyard, etc. *Chipolas* are like little vegetable containers.

Noche de fiero chubasco. A *chubasco* is rain and strong wind together. (Words for rain: *chubasco, aguacero, chaparrón, garúa.*) The wet season brings storms, lightning, thunder, floods, rivers in spate, full of tree trunks, animals, vegetation of all sorts: very noisy and terrifying.

El capacho is the tree from whose gourds and seeds maracas are made. *Bordón:* the deeper strings of the harp. *Vena en corazón de cedro:* heart of cedar, the gut strings imagined as veins. *Caramera,* antlers: dead deer or perhaps a simile for dead trees, their branches in the air… Mines in the Llanos: a puzzling reference.

Canta una voz sabanera: a high-pitched voice that carries in the wind, calling to men and cattle. On evenings of song, the rum flows. This well-primed singer is probably not Florentino.

Cimarrones: wild cattle survive very easily on the abundant grass. Riders go out in expeditions to *picarlos,* gee them back to the herd. *Orejano:* unbranded cattle. *Guerras federales*: internecine wars of much bloodshed and suffering between the landed classes, *godos*, and the *federales* or liberals. Here is a relevant account:

> "Joining forces at Guanare [capital of an adjacent state] in mid-November 1859, the generals Falcón and Zamora (liberals/federals) headed for Barinas, followed by the government's western army (conservatives/'goths') under general Ramos, whose orders were to pursue and defeat them. The retreating federals took position at the village of Santa Inés, located some 36 kms south-east of Barinas City, on the right bank of the Santo Domingo River."

Barinas borders the Andean States, its terrain rising gently to the west. Santa Inés is located on the first slopes, so the singer calls it *montaña de Santa Inés:* the proper llanos are flat as pancakes. The term *godos* 'goths' recalls those invaders who ruled much of Spain, centuries ago.

149-227 *Indio de grave postura:* an Amerindian. These original inhabitants of *los llanos* are not, strictly speaking, llaneros; the cattlemen are of thoroughly mixed race (see below). To 'conquer' the llanos, the Catholic Church sent its *avanzadas* of missionaries to convert the scattered Amerindians, gather them in a *fundación* to work as well as pray, and then claim the land. Usually, the farmers would follow. Sometimes the Church was keen to keep the land, thousands of hectares at a time, and disputes ensued until the Jesuits were expelled in the 19th century and the *godo* landowners took over. The Amerindians had lived undisturbed for centuries before the interference of the white people, and of the escaped African slaves in their free communes, *cumbias*. The Amerindians are of ancient times. They are famously quiet and enigmatic, keep to themselves, and have a strong sense of who they are.

Faja: a strong cloth round the waist. The red blood mole is a sinister touch. *Jeme,* from Latin *semis:* half a foot long. This dagger measures a *jeme* and a half. Gold teeth: a source of pride. *Nutrias* (Waterdogs, Otters) is an important town on the Apure river, the chief entrance to the *Llanos* for travellers by water.

Florentino plays the harp. The fingers of his right hand play the higher strings of this diatonic, celtic, triangular harp, improvising the melody in *sol menor*, G minor, and the fingers of the left hand rein them in. *El indio pico de oro:* When someone is a good orator in Venezuela they will say: *tiene pico de plata*, he has a silver beak.

The Devil opens by addressing Florentino as *catire*, blond: *catire quita pesares*. *Quitapesares* is a form of *joropo*; it also literally means 'sorrow-stopper'. It is not unusual for *llaneros* to be blond and have yellow/greenish eyes, from some wandering European gene. The *llanero* Juan Antonio Páez, one of the heroes of Independence and a renowned singer and composer, was called El Catire Páez. By calling Florentino 'catire', the Devil establishes the difference between them, maybe even his ascendancy over him, an *indio* taking precedence over a modern *llanero*. *Quita pesares* here means light-hearted, cheerful (is Florentino being teased for his melancholy?). The Devil, who is the challenger and has taken the lead, will first ask five questions. Florentino must reply repeating his last line and rhyming from it, and the Devil must do the same before setting the next question: it's the rule of this type of *contrapunteo*. Eventually, the replies will no longer be in quatrains but get longer and longer as the poetic inspiration takes flight with fine metaphors and similes. The first question takes us to the cock-fighting ring and seems an eternal one: what is the secret of victory? Being hit on the beak is a serious matter but if he cock follows certain golden rules, it may turn that wound to its advantage. Florentino's reply, which is said to be the epitome of cockfighting wisdom, is much used in a political context: President Chávez, for example, was portrayed as the tough guy, the fighting-cock from Barinas that triumphs over a very refined cockerel from Caracas. Florentino replies that the cock should overcome the other's attack without confronting it, without opposing the adversary's strength. The cock is good if it strikes the feet but better *si agarra en la pluma*. This is a more complex move: the cock hits and holds the other by a feather of its chest, and pivoting strikes the head with its spur ((often aiming at the eye): strategy rather than force. The Devil picks up the last line and asks his second question, which, funnily enough, is a pseudo-political one, much reflecting the way the Republic, after 1830, was managed, the stronger pillaging the country at every opportunity. Which is the ideal republic where booty is won with no effort and no danger? Florentino's reply goes back to nature: a honeycomb in the papaya tree. The trunk is short and thin, the fruit is easy to reach. If you don't carry a machete to cut the honeycomb, you can still get the honey out with your nails. The third question, as we are in *los llanos*, is musical. What are the four rivers that are silent if no one crosses them and sonorous when someone does? Florentino is quick to identify the four strings of the Spanish guitarrilla that became so popular in Venezuela, the cuatro in colonial times: it was smaller and easier to carry on horseback than a big guitar. The cuatro has little resonance, the fingers of the right hand must strum continuously over the strings while those of the left hand, nearer the chest and the *traste* fret, move up and down, changing the note at enormous speed: *salpica el tono en el traste como en la piedra la espuma*. And now Florentino introduces another move in the game of contrapunteo: *la repregunta*: he makes a derisive comment on the Devil's wit. It's as if he is saying: with this kind of easy question, you are giving me room to play cat and mouse with you, and I'll confuse you.

229-251 The Devil's fourth question is about riding, another passion and special skill of the *llanero*. The answer is too easy: the Devil should know better. *Jamugas* are a sort of basket or woven bag; a *matadura* is a nasty insect-bite, which the boy only has to tickle and the poor animal trots faster.

In the fifth question, the Devil wants to show Florentino the power he already has over him, and humiliate him in front of the audience. He wants him to confess that he, the Devil, stopped him from drinking water, on the night of their first encounter.

Veneno: the Indians put a paralysing poison on their arrow-heads to make a monkey fall in the middle of a jump from branch to branch, so it is much easier to retrieve.

252-265 Florentino replies in terms of warfare. El Catire Páez and his men, *sus lanceros*, famously used to catch a spear in flight and return it against the thrower. They would also run away from the enemy and at the last moment, turn round (*¡vuelvan caras!*) and spear them ruthlessly. This is what Florentino is doing, catching the poisoned weapon and hurling it back at the Devil. He mercilessly lets everyone know that the Devil can never drink water (whereas he himself was unable only on that night). First he paints an extraordinarily condensed image of *la sequía*, the drought, to emphasize the torture of being a creature, devil or no devil, that can never assuage such monstrous thirst. He uses in sequence four prepositions (*sobre, bajo, por, en*) that have an enveloping effect: *sobre suelos errantes* could suggest dust clouds again, under the thirsty dunes, by salty waters (a *llanero* does not know the sea, but Florentino may have travelled to the coast)... *En el mar de estas llanuras*: the heat waves, or the inmensity of the plains, when even the air is burning (the sap boiling, the sigh of burning wind) and the lochan is seared, *se tuesta la laguna:* in those terrible circumstances, he who never drinks water must drink sand. Point made.

266-295 The Devil will not be fobbed off. A straight answer, please, to that episode of the sand! *Brusca*, a medicinal plant, will weaken the coffee and send the guests home early from the wake, *velorio*. He rephrases the question. But Florentino sings of the deep lonesome dunes, or of a man's heart. He vaunts his art with a stock phrase of the *contrapunteo*: he who seeks me, finds me.

296-313 The Devil counters with a list of ominous and horrid sounds growing louder and louder until cockcrow, when Florentino will be reduced to silence. From here onwards there are twenty-two names of birds. Birds are prominent in *llanero* songs, and famous singers take names of birds like *turpial, carrao*... 'El Carrao de Palmarito', a great exponent, can be heard singing the Devil on YouTube. Nestor Zavarce is 'El Pájaro Chogüí'; Héctor Hernández is 'El Gabán'.

314-325 Florentino retorts that the dawn finds him clear-headed and in good voice. Like the troupial, the black-and-yellow national bird, he sings better against a rival; like the scented buckthorn, he hurts those who give him trouble.

326-381 The Devil says the buckthorn is menaced by fire, flood, insects, drought and hurricanes. [*bachaco*: a big red ant that nests in the sap of the buckthorn.] Hurricanes may flap the flag, Florentino tells him, yet the mast stays strong. If you can't cope with this, you'd best keep quiet: don't stutter and flutter, don't be a pathetic panhandler, a clueless cattleman, a cheesecake chump, a woman told off by another... Hark at those bass notes!—Hah, says the Devil, I'll show you some real skill on the harp, I can sharpen the spurs on a fighting-cock, make sure it wins... Come where you can see me. Face me!

[386 *'colea'*: two riders, chasing a bull at a gallop, compete to catch it by the tail and, by overtaking it, bring it down.]

382-411 Don't ride too near the bull, says Florentino: I come at it straight, you swerve across. A *llanero* can ride front or back: front man pressing on, back man at ease. —Back man can't see what's coming to him, says the Devil: I enjoy singing outdoors on a stormy night against a frogs' chorus: we can tell who sings better!

412-437 F: The best singer-poet just does his job on the ranch and minds his own business. And I will not be going outside to sing in the dark.

438-471 D: You are now under my harsh law. I am not lenient with debtors. You are a slack believer, you ignore the saints until your boat capsizes.

F: Good preacher, bad singer! Read this if you can: for all the dust you raise, I have the light of reason to see by. Feeble kicks from Molly, the tame, harmless mule!

473-536 D: Bucking jackass, you won't throw me easily. Relax, have some rum, you'll need it.

F: Don't you worry! I don't eat with you, I don't care what you eat, I don't care whether you sing or dry up.

D: You'll dry up when you lose heart. Pretty speeches won't do, they vanish like train-smoke: a poet must tread hot earth, kick up dust!

F: A fire stops at the green river-bank. A jackass can't play the flute. No-one ties me down. I can pick out a feral bull, or one that's tame but still unbranded, among hundreds. I am honest, I keep no smuggled goods.

D: It's hard to read a business deal, to know who's come out on top; it's hard to read the reaction of a courted girl. We shall see if your voice falters, when you're damned.

537 F: With my cuatro and the maracas, I'm in control, I'm free. I needn't drink from anyone's gourd, needn't bare my arms to midges. I'm in control because I'm a singer who can also play the music: I can sing when I please.

551 D: So proud, and in stormy weather! I'm not here to give you cakes. I'll show you who I am, by the scale of my works. I sculpt the hills, I covet the mountains! I contrive weakness and failure. You are nervy, so you are malicious! And no wonder: after a snakebite, you're scared of a liana.

569 F: Your toffee bullets don't scare me. You run your mill, I'll run mine. I can't be bullied. I'm not brittle timber! Women are good to me: ever since I rolled cobnuts [played marbles as a lad], on dark nights I've seen the May Cross in heaven.

591 D: Shadows don't scare me. I'm a hawk, a fierce owl, a curlew, a great ibis; I'm a scorpion, a slippery fish, a roaring monkey, a watchful cayman.

609 F: I can deal with you: I shoot the bird as it turns, harpoon the cayman, hook the slimy fish. A ninny can't ride bareback; you can't dry your face without a hanky; bare feet don't need washing. [*Implied: you are shoeless and homeless.*]

629 D: (*Insulted, declares victory.*) A man with his ear to the ground can sleep safely. It's cockcrow! Fly, my black vultures! Gentlemen: *I've got him.*

642 F: I didn't agree to anything. Plovers, ibises, lend me your wings, keep it going, he's flagging. If he says I am his, then I am the vendor: he must pay up at once! I'm not a soft touch, a flood-plain farmer, a booby-bird warming another's nest.

659 D: You're an exhausted sculler, losing the rhythm. Your top note [*their sustained, wordless high tenor A*] will be silenced.

669 F: I don't take you seriously, nor your boasts about what you may have done. I ask no more than my due.

683 D: You are my debtor and I've done all the necessary. Your time is up.

697 F: It's always early when I'm singing. I love the rain and thunder and the beauty of the plains. You can't silence me. Open-necked—you'll catch cold!

719 D: Your jokes won't put me off: I'm a master-poet. I blacken the crops, I wear the evil badge of death, I never forget.

733 F: I recall glow-worms *[fireflies]* threading the oaks with pinpoints of dew. I take stock, I have desire and longing. I retain what I teach, I forget what I learn.

751 D: Wind and cloud, desolation, storm and lightning are mine. I pierce wild bulls' noses, I tame them, they shudder. *He perhaps touches his dagger, or even draws it.)*

763 F: Give me space to teach one who thinks a man can be scared like a beast. Draw your dagger…? (*He may make the same gesture.*) I don't go down without a fight.

779 D: A proud loser! I shall take you down. The long boat is coming to bring you pain and doom.

'AMBUSH'. *At line 796, the Devil abruptly changes the rhyme from −io to −é. At line 974 he will abruptly change it from −é to −ajo. At 1071, Florentino will retaliate, going from −ajo to −á−.*

800 F: I'm a free spirit and I love the music of Apure and Barinas.

[The Pagüey river flows through the state of Barinas into the Apure river, beyond which is the state of Apure. The troupial is a kind of oriole, black and yellow, a great songbird and the national bird of Venezuela.]

808 D: I can handle a boat in tricky waters.

816 F: A likely tale! You don't exactly smell of roses.

824 D: *(Sorry for himself)* One alone paints the flowers. I wish I could flower.

832 F: Blossoms fall in the dry season and return with the rain.

840 D: There's a place with no flower, no verdure, no rain, but only thirst.

848 F: At my cabin it's cool by the samán tree and the water.

858 D: *(Recovers)* Not when the waters recede [in November] and the birds come crowding, the ducks in pairs, the herons in flocks: then the moon is bereft, the plants die, the livestock drinks no more.

868 F: That's too mundane for me! I have my star, my eternal faith.

876 D: Your star is a sorry drudge, and eternity is the common lot, sombre as life, bitter as laurel.

886 F: Laurels die in dry weather, but in May in the plains, the *bucare* and the *araguaney* are in bloom. In the humble hearth, I see a great light.

[*Bucare*: a spiny shade-tree, Erythrina poeppigiana, salmon-pink. *Araguaney*: the national tree of Venezuela, tabebuia chrysanthus, yellow.]

898 D: A great light? I was cut down at the root. I work mischief! To the proud, I bring sorrow with no waking.

910 F: Good sense wakes at five o'clock, the brave world wakes at six, when life is blessed by the herd in the pen and the wisp of coffee.

920 D: Would-be jovial bard, your faith and pride are broken! You are tamed! People in bad times want gold or honey, not your doggerel.

934 F: Clouds cast no shadow on one who tells and tallies only the good, not the bad: and the best tale will be for you, when dawn breaks at Santa Inés.

946 D: I knew you'd be skilled and fearless, a corsair with my boat's crew, a leader, a man of wine and women. You wear the laurel of—failure!

956 F: I say my prayers, to thwart the one who cannot drink water, unless he traces the Cross.

965 D: I'm given cobs with no corn, I can't drink from the river. I swerve with the smoke that lures like tinfoil: I change course, can you follow?

[*He switches the rhyme from –é to –ajo: more difficult. The translator sustains a repeated –ning. At 992 the Devil resorts to puns on –ajo words.*]

978 F: If you chose clarinet, don't play contrabass, don't clank cymbals like a cart on rubble. Not every line is verse, or makes a rhyme for garlic-skinning; the knack of bell-ringing is not in hanging from the clapper. Art is discipline, even in heaven: if an archangel goes out of tune, it's the conductor straying.

992 D: It's the conductor straying, musing on puns.

[*escofina*, a rasp for hooves; *estropajo*, a gourd like a loofah. 'File a hoof, love a loofah' might be a whimsical saying of the *llaneros*, if they spoke English. *marrajo*, cunning; *amarra ajos*, 'one who ties up garlic,' in order to improve the crop. This is not done by the large producers.]

I've crumpled legal documents, I respect the poorly-dressed. My singing thrills, unnerves and outwits my opponent. I crush but don't shame him, I trounce without spurning.

[*This is a favourite couplet of politicians when they win elections.*]

1010 F: In a fight, I don't torture, nor do I flatter. It's me or the tiger, as there's no calf to feed the brute. You rain blows on me, of course I hit back. I took you on, as you took me on: I'm holding my own. Black vultures, here's a salesman who didn't salt the beef! Now, sirs, the Devil's in trouble!

1032 D: Don't lie: you don't know me: don't pretend to be unscathed. These people know the harm I wreak. I suck a little lime dry, segment by segment.

1048 F: No worries, my friends! Let him set up his rodeo, I'll turn it loose. Before daybreak, the one who brought him here shall remove him. The fine horse will lead the skulking donkey. When the lamp of morning shines, he changed the rhyme, so can I.

[1065 *se lo lleva*... a reminder, as at line 827, that the Devil is subject to a higher power. *Dorodoro*, local word for a vulture: these can only hiss and grunt. *Arrendajo llanero*, an energetic songbird, brilliant black with yellow trim, called *cacique*, chieftain: it can be found on YouTube at mp4, xexéu. ...At 1071, Florentino switches the rhyme from –ajo to –a-.]

1075 D: *[self-pitying, as at 830,969]* High notes, low notes, crowded or lonely, I don't care. I gave up the infallible for the uncertain, I gave up repose for trouble. I sustain my ancient grudge.

1087 F: *[again dwells on birds and on the higher power.]*

1103 D: Your dismal trail... No scarlet ibis, no ring dove...

[*Corocora, the scarlet ibis, a truly spectacular bird. La Corocora de los llanos, stage name of the Colombian singer Virginia Rocha. Torcaz, wood pigeon, ring dove:* torquatus.]

No eaves, no embers: *no sociable shelter, no campfires.*

1119 F: I am above board. *[Arvelo was a lawyer.]* My possessions are what I give, my name is the name given me, my home is where I go, I pay my way.

1139 D: My strap is on your muzzle: you're on your way already! No good to you rhyme and song, no good to you love and faith and skill. Songbird!

[1149 *Qué delito...* this obscure line interferes with the rhyme-scheme: it may be a gloss, not part of the original text: or else the next line is missing.]

1166 F: You'll walk a poor, waterless path. I have the light flooding in, I sing through the storm, I steer by the refrain. You're not the captain in command.

1182 D: You are a fallen sail... the Captain of Darkness is coming for you.

1198 F: Pleased to meet you, Mr Satan. Evil birds, come and tint your black wings in the sunrise! The Devil has failed!

1212 D: No art will save you. Vampire bats on your face foretell your pain in the Suffering City.

1224 F: You can't supervise my gaming: I am of full age. I place my own bets. I have never squandered the good things of life...

1244 D: The waters are closing on you. Sigh farewell to light and love and faith, take thought, consider. Who will cry the deep cry? Why is lying a crime, when the truth is worse? Sigh farewell to time: he who strove for eternity shall eternally suffer. Sigh farewell to the Cross, and to that, give no thought.

[Much sighing: the imperative suspire *is followed by* suspirar *with five different imperatives.]*

1268 F: O rescue me, with God's aid, Our Lady... [*of Solitude; of Carmel...* Our Lady of Carmel, patron of the sea in Spain, of the army in Venezuela; the blest Virgin of El Real, patron of Barinas; Our Lady of Succour; Our Lady of Peace, patron of the nearby town of Trujillo; Our Lady of Lourdes in France. Our Lady of Coromoto, patron of Venezuela since 1942, appeared to a local chief in 1652 and left him a small painting, now in a huge basilica. Our Lady of Chiquinquirá, patron of Maracaibo, appeared as a wooden tablet to a woman washing in that lake. The Virgin of the Vale is patron of the Island of Margarita. The Virgin of the Pillar appeared in AD 40 to St James the Greater in Zaragoza, Spain, 'in mortal flesh' before her Assumption, leaving a pillar of jasper. Our Lady of Sorrows is represented weeping, her heart emitting rays of light. The Archangel Michael is a warrior; the Holy Child of Atocha is the young Jesus who succoured captives near 13th-century Madrid. Finally, Florentino calls on the Holy Trinity.]

1297: [*They say the Devil went back to the poet Alberto Arvelo, claiming that Florentino had cheated by invoking divine powers, and wanting the contest to continue...*]

TRANSLATOR'S NOTE ON THE RHYMING

The cattlemen of Venezuela's plains have a magnificent tradition of ballads, composed impromptu and sung in man-to-man contest. Quickfire rhymes are repeatedly echoed and suddenly changed. A translation can hardly do the same, but by copious rhyme and assonance I hope to have conveyed the intricacy of Arvelo's original. This tussle for a human soul is sung in various versions on YouTube.

In the Spanish text, every other line is rhymed. The same rhyming vowel, or vowel pattern, is used with unvarying persistence for at least seventy lines (35 couplets) running, often many more.

— In lines 1 to 99, the rhyming vowel is always **é**, most often followed by some consonant which may vary.

— On reaching Santa Inés at line 100, we have a feminine rhyme until line 299: **u-a**, stressed **u** followed by unstressed **a**, with a choice of consonants, or maybe none, in between.

— Then at line 300 'The Devil changes the rhyme' and until line 481 it is **–ea**, with no consonant in between: again, a feminine rhyme.

— *'The Poet sings and plays...* ¡Ay, catire Florentino!'

— The Devil is just four lines into his next speech when he abruptly changes the rhyme to **–ene(s)** for lines 482 to 559. At 561, again four lines into a speech, he changes abruptly to **–elo** which persists to line 635.

— At this point he is confident enough to call for a toast. He switches to **–ío** which persists to line 800.

— Now we are warned *'Ambush'* and The Devil gives Florentino just three lines' notice of the next rhyme, again **–é**, which persists to line 978.

— Again he gives just three lines notice and we have the very demanding –**ajo** which persists to 1074, giving rise to some far-fetched images. Finally it's Florentino's turn to alter the rhyme at three lines' notice, to –á, most often followed by a consonant, which takes us through to the end at 1302, Santísima Trinidá.

In the English text, it would be impracticable to repeat the same rhyme for so many couplets on end, while staying faithful to the meaning. The lines are short, the rhymes are frequent, and besides, it is less easy to rhyme in English than in Spanish. However, when the Spanish text has the difficult –*ajo* rhyme, with some far-fetched results such as the loofah and the beetle, I have managed to sustain a series of feminine rhymes ending in –*ning*.

Lightning Source UK Ltd.
Milton Keynes UK
UKOW05f0100251014

240564UK00001B/74/P